A CONVENIENT DEATH

A CONVENIENT DEATH

The Mysterious Demise of Jeffrey Epstein

Alana Goodman and Daniel Halper

SENTINEL

Sentinel
An imprint of Penguin Random House LLC
penguinrandomhouse.com

Most Sentinel books are available at a discount when purchased in quantity for sales promotions or corporate use. Special editions, which include personalized covers, excerpts, and corporate imprints, can be created when purchased in large quantities. For more information, please call (212) 572- 2232 or e-mail specialmarkets@penguinrandomhouse .com. Your local bookstore can also assist with discounted bulk purchases using the Penguin Random House corporate Business-to-Business program. For assistance in locating a participating retailer, e-mail B2B@penguinrandomhouse.com.

ISBN 9780593853955 (paperback)
ISBN 9780593192245 (ebook)

Book design by Cassandra Garruzzo

147141878

To my grandfather,
the brilliant writer Herbert Post (z"l).
We all miss you every day.

ALANA GOODMAN

To my girls,
who provide bright light in a very dark world:
Joanna, Eve, Ruby.

DANIEL HALPER

When I was 15 years old, I flew on Jeffrey Epstein's plane to Zorro Ranch, where I was sexual[ly] molested by him for many hours. What I remember most vividly was him explaining to me how beneficial the experience was for me and how much he was helping me to grow. I remember feeling so small and powerless, especially after he positioned me by laying me on his floor so that I was confronted by all the framed photographs on his dresser of him smiling with wealthy celebrities and politicians.

JANE DOE #9[1]

CONTENTS

PART II
An Indecent Life

INTRODUCTION

Conspiracy theories spring up when an official story is implausible, unpersuasive, or, sometimes, total bunk. These days they seem to develop on the margins of the internet and then spread to the general public—often very, very quickly. The best are not made up out of whole cloth. They are carefully considered alternative theories to understand something that does not make sense. They rely on facts, or at least kernels of truth, which are then expanded and extrapolated on to come somewhere, somehow closer to telling a more complete and (one hopes) truthful story.

So, what happens when a conspiracy theory comes true? That is what seemed to happen on August 10, 2019, when one of the most notorious inmates ever to inhabit the Metropolitan Correctional Center was found hanging in his cell.

Ever since Jeffrey Epstein, notorious pedophile and pal/client to the rich and famous, was arrested, people had speculated that he would be murdered. Over the years, Epstein had befriended some of the most powerful men in the world—presidents, princes, business titans—embroiling many of them in his sex scandals. As he awaited trial, many people mused that he had more secrets to share, more scandals to expose, perhaps more powerful names to implicate. What would happen if he decided to squeal? Worse, for his powerful allies, would he be so desperate to get out of jail that he would be willing to tell authorities whatever they wanted to hear just for the chance to be free? Would they risk this possibility, or would they ensure that he could not expose them?

"If Epstein talks, there's gonna be a lot of powerful people who could go down," Nick Bryant, a dogged reporter who had been on the Epstein case for far longer than just about everyone else, speculated in an interview.[1]

The *Miami Herald* reporter Julie K. Brown went a little further in her detailing of the "very powerful people" close to Epstein. "They're sweating a little bit, especially today," Brown told MSNBC the day after Epstein was arrested. "There have been a lot of names that I could see on these message pads [listing clients] on a regular basis as part of the evidence. These message pads where they would call and leave Epstein messages, such as, 'I'm at this hotel.' Why do you do that, unless you're expecting him to send you a girl to visit you at your hotel? So there are probably quite a few important people, powerful people, who are sweating it out right now. We'll have to wait and see whether Epstein is going to name names."[2]

Epstein's sudden, unexpected death brought that to a most convenient end. It ensured those secrets were never revealed, that so many questions would never be answered. To his accomplices and abettors, his would have been the most timely and useful suicide ever committed.

If that's really what it was. Questions about whether the notorious sex offender had been murdered arose within minutes once the news of his death reached the public.

Even President Donald Trump, a former friend of Epstein's, re-tweeted a Twitter message from one of his supporters that speculated Epstein "had information on Bill Clinton & now he's dead."

"I see #TrumpBodyCount trending but we know who did this!" said the Twitter post.

As reporters who have, between us, covered plenty of news stories and unsubstantiated conspiracy theories, we have become natural skeptics. We've learned to take with a grain of salt wild accusations or in some cases wishful thinking, even when they come from the president of the United States. But as we began to look into the Epstein story, we started to understand the widespread skepticism. The official story of Epstein's death had holes in it—big holes—from the beginning. Cameras that might have chronicled the scene mysteriously failed. Tapes were suddenly erased, disappearing, or someway inoperable.

Reasonable questions multiplied. Why were the guards at that cellblock so lax, especially when dealing with such a notorious and high-profile cellmate? Why were the security cameras so error prone at this particular moment? Was this really just a jailhouse "comedy of errors" with a distinctly unfunny ending? How could a prison that housed some of the most deadly and dangerous criminals in the nation really behave so unprofessionally, so sloppily? Or was there something more going on?

No one has done a good job answering these questions. Not the feds. Not any state government. Not New York City officials. Not the media. Not Jeffrey Epstein's friends and associates—and there are many—who themselves are still enjoying life from their perch at the upper echelon of our political, elite class. An August 2019 public poll conducted by Emerson College found that 34 percent of Americans believed that Epstein had been murdered.[3] By January 2020, 52 percent of Americans believed he was "murdered to prevent him from testifying against powerful people with whom he associated."

INTRODUCTION

As we looked into the case for ourselves, we kept turning up more questions to answer, more suspicions to explore, more new facts that emerged to fill the gaps and challenge the official narrative. We examined the mystery of his finances and his secretive business arrangements. We interviewed those who knew Jeffrey Epstein well, either as friends, business or legal associates, or because they were victimized by him.

A Convenient Death will not help you trust media accounts of Epstein's death. It will not restore your faith in the government or other powerful American institutions.

What it will do is take readers inside the dark corners of the American and international power structure, revealing why any number of people could have been driven to drastic action to make sure those corners stayed in the shadows. And it will make readers uncomfortable, especially those who believe there is nothing to be learned from Epstein's crime spree and the complete mishandling of justice.

In part 1, "The Death," we tell the story of Jeffrey Epstein's final weeks, days, and hours. We examine the evidence he left behind. We lay out the problems with the official narrative, and through our exclusive interviews and never-before-revealed reporting we address the lingering questions that perplexed so many Americans. As you'll see, the closer sources were to the story, the less they were likely to believe that Epstein had committed suicide. They believed that was not his style. Not part of his ethos. And that it would be a bit too convenient for him.

In part 2, "An Indecent Life," we tell the stories of some of the rich and famous who considered Epstein a friend and colleague. We also examine Epstein's life and consider who, if anyone, might have benefited from his mysterious demise.

We would like to include a brief note before the story begins. Both of us are investigative political reporters with wide-ranging experience breaking news on sensitive and uncomfortable political subjects. Jeffrey Epstein's life, and death, is certainly one of those areas. Readers should be aware that the facts reported in the following pages are based exclusively on conversations with direct sources, primary court and public records documents, and published media accounts.

We have extensively interviewed those who knew Epstein and his alleged accomplices and victims, individuals who worked at the prison where he died, and those who investigated his shocking and unexpected death.

We came to this case with fresh eyes and open minds. In the end the story is much worse and more pernicious than even we believed. Epstein's story isn't just about Epstein; it's about the horrifying misdeeds of the elite and of those who covered up their corruption. The powerful may not want you to know these stories, but it's time Americans learned the truth.

PART I
The Death

1
Final Hours

To the day he died, he never thought he did anything wrong.

ALAN DERSHOWITZ

Ten days before Jeffrey Epstein's death, the reception area on the third floor of the Metropolitan Correctional Center was buzzing with activity. Lawyers carrying legal pads shuffled in and out of the second conference room from the left, aggravating the desk guard who had to walk over every time and unlock the door.

The conference room was barely bigger than a prison cell, with just enough space for a cheap wooden table and five chairs. The only window overlooked the reception area, where the guard kept watch from his desk. There were no laptops or cell phones allowed. Occasionally, one of the attorneys would step out and relay a message to a couple of young female lawyers camped in the waiting area. The women, a pair of attractive recent law school grads, were couriers for Jeffrey Epstein. They, for an hourly fee, also kept him company between his meetings.

Inside the room, holding court, was Epstein. The sixty-six-year-old multimillionaire, silver-haired and well-built from daily exercise, had been in jail for nearly a month on charges of sex trafficking underage girls. Most of his days were spent in this conference room, a designated area for legal meetings. He looked good—healthy, even—in his prison-issued orange jumpsuit and matching socks. On this particular day, August 1, 2019, he seemed upbeat and focused as his lawyers circulated in and out. Today was an important day for him, a day he hoped to take his first big step toward legal victory and freedom and away from a place where he was miserable.

Epstein, a germaphobe and lifelong teetotaler, hated the indignities of MCC—the roaches, the rodents, the drug addicts. His current cellmate was a "junkie" who "smoked crack in the cell," he complained to friends. He was also fearful of other prisoners due to his great wealth, upwards of $500 million, including real estate. His finances were splashed all over the news—"$56 Million Upper East Side Mansion"—and he worried about getting shaken down by protection rackets.[1] He had reportedly started paying off other inmates through their commissary accounts.

In the afternoon, the prison psychologist stopped by for a ten-minute counseling session. The previous month, Epstein had been placed on twenty-four-hour suicide watch after prison guards found him unconscious in his cell. (Epstein denied that there had been a suicide attempt, but he was certainly not happy in prison.) He was removed from suicide watch after six days, on July 29, but he was still under psychological monitoring.

After the therapy session, Epstein met with his friend and lawyer David Schoen, who he believed was his key to getting out. Epstein had known Schoen, a balding, bespectacled sixty-one-year-old Alabama civil rights attorney, for more than a decade. Both men liked to trash-talk and had a distinct contempt for authority. They had grown closer over the past year, and Epstein often reached out to Schoen for legal advice.

Today Epstein had a bigger ask. He wanted to restructure his legal team and bring Schoen on board. It was an important step, one that he thought would help refocus his talented but disorganized camp of lawyers, putting them in a good position for the fight ahead. Moreover, he faced a curious problem: he felt let down by some of his more high-profile lawyers and betrayed because he did not believe they were fighting hard enough for him. He had seen how anyone associated with him had taken a public beating. Epstein had never been completely immune to or unaware of the public lashing he received. And yet he had no sympathy for the lawyers who would gladly cash his big checks and at the same time not sufficiently fight for him or, worse, were embarrassed to be associated with him. He needed someone who was fully on his side and asked Schoen to take the lead on trial preparation.

Epstein's trial date had been set for the following June, nearly a year away. His legal team believed they needed at least that much time to prepare for the complex case and review more than a million pages of discovery materials that prosecutors were expected to turn over.

Schoen said he was willing to come on board. The two men agreed to reconvene the week of August 12 to move forward on preparing for the trial. In the meantime, Schoen, who lived in Atlanta, planned to relocate part-time to New York for the duration of the case and began setting up a team of lawyers, too.

Schoen's support thrilled Epstein and gave him hope. Finally he was going to elevate the lawyer who would stand tall next to him and be willing to accept the public blowback for being associated with him.

"He was very upbeat," recalled Schoen. "He didn't want to be charged, but if he was, he was going to fight it all the way."

—

The Metropolitan Correctional Center, where the disgraced mogul spent his final days, is a twelve-story cinder-block building near the foot of the Brooklyn Bridge in lower Manhattan. Built in 1975 by Gruzen & Partners—the same design firm that built the posh Solow Tower condo building that Epstein lived in as an investment banker in the 1980s—the prison embodies that decade's brutalist architecture, with its poured-concrete walls and stark rectangular towers. The windows are made of thick shatterproof plastic with no obvious bars. There is no ground-level yard or security fence. From the outside, it could be mistaken for an aging government office building.

There, Epstein awaited his federal trial at the penitentiary that previously safely housed drug lords (El Chapo), mafiosi (John Gotti), terrorists (al-Qaeda operatives), Ponzi schemers (Bernie Madoff), and fraudsters (Paul Manafort).[2] Epstein was incarcerated in the Special Housing Unit, a wing known as 9-South. The section is largely reserved for inmates in protective custody or who had been placed there for disciplinary purposes.

Epstein, a self-described money manager from Coney Island who claimed to work exclusively for billionaires and had built a fortune, was facing up to forty-five years in prison on underage sex trafficking charges. According to prosecutors, Epstein had recruited and sexually abused dozens of teenage girls at his houses in Manhattan and Palm Beach between 2002 and 2005. This was his second arrest for sex crimes; he was previously convicted of soliciting and procuring underage prostitutes in 2008. But the prior case had involved state charges in Florida, and Epstein had been able to cut a deal for a lenient sentence in a work-release program. This time, he was facing federal charges in the U.S. District Court for the Southern District of New York.

"The victims, who were as young as 14 years of age, were told by Epstein or other individuals to partially or fully undress before beginning the 'massage,'" according to the July 2019 federal indictment.[3] "During the encounter, Epstein would escalate the nature and scope of physical contact with his victim to include, among other things, sex acts such as groping and direct or indirect contact with the victim's genitals.

"Epstein would typically also masturbate during these sexualized encounters, ask victims to touch him while he masturbated, and touch victims' genitals with his hands or sex toys," said the indictment. "Victims were typically paid hundreds of dollars in cash for each encounter."

Epstein's legal issues had already caused problems for his powerful political friends. His looming high-profile trial could be an even greater liability.

The former president Bill Clinton was being hammered in the press for taking multiple trips on Epstein's private Boeing 727, nicknamed the Lolita Express.[4] Prince Andrew's position in the royal family was in jeopardy after photos emerged of him with his hand around the waist of one of Epstein's alleged underage "sex slaves." President Donald Trump was being scrutinized for his social outings with Epstein in the 1990s, and a handful of other political figures—the former senator George Mitchell, the former governor Bill Richardson, and the former Israeli prime minister Ehud Barak—also faced allegations for their involvement with Epstein.

But Epstein had no intention of going down quietly. He did not believe he had done anything wrong.

"His theory was always that sixteen-, seventeen-, eighteen-year-olds are having sex with their boyfriends," said Alan Dershowitz, the high-profile defense attorney who represented Epstein off and on for years, in an interview. "So, what's the big deal? They made $250. They gave him a massage. He masturbated. That's the end of it. He didn't think he ruined anybody's life. He never thought he did anything wrong. To the day he died, he never thought he did anything wrong. He thought that the culture was all screwed up about sex and young women."

Epstein's lawyers were confident of his chances. They believed the federal case against him was "pretty weak" due to several factors. First, Epstein had already entered a non-prosecution agreement with the Department of Justice more than a decade earlier that allowed him to plead guilty to state charges in Florida and avoid federal prosecution in that district. Because the latest charges involved some of the same incidents and victims, they argued that the federal government's Department of Justice was not allowed to retry him in another state.

Second, Epstein's lawyers felt they could make an argument for double jeopardy based on the prior prosecution. Finally, they thought the government had flimsy evidence when it came to interstate transportation of the girls, the key basis for bringing a federal indictment.

"He had a pretty good case," said Dershowitz. "Although the deck was stacked against him because he was Jeffrey Epstein, he might very well have won the case."

—

Epstein might have had another reason to feel he could get off easy.

When the feds raided his Manhattan mansion after his arrest in early July, they found "a vast trove of lewd photographs of young-looking women or girls." The photographs were locked up and highly organized. It amounted to child pornography. But it may also have been something else: blackmail, featuring not just young, innocent children but also the perpetrators.

It is unclear how Epstein acquired his photo stash, but friends said he had an extensive video surveillance system throughout his house in New York. Everything was monitored—the guest bedrooms, the bathrooms.

"There were cameras everywhere," said one longtime friend in an interview. "Why? That's good evidence that he's a blackmailer, and it's good evidence that he has some bad stuff on people."

—

Meanwhile, Epstein continued his daily monopoly of one of the third-floor legal conference rooms, which were technically supposed to be available to all inmates on a first-come basis. He filled his time with various legal matters. On Thursday, August 8, Epstein's financial attorneys established a trust in the Virgin Islands to house his assets. The move shielded the full scope of his fortune and created more legal hurdles for accusers who sued him for damages. Epstein also signed a new copy of his last will and testament that would transfer his $577 million fortune in disclosed assets to the trust in the event of his death.

The next day, August 9, Epstein met with his defense lawyers in the cramped third-floor conference room to talk trial strategy. By all accounts he was in a fighting mood, "just barking out orders with all the stuff that I had told them we need to start working on," said Schoen, who was back in Atlanta for the Jewish sabbath but received a readout after the meeting. "He [was] so excited about going forward."

The team planned to file an appeal motion the following Monday to try to get him out on bail—a fairly long shot. His lawyers were more confident about other avenues they were pursuing, such as their attempts to get the case tossed due to the non-prosecution agreement Epstein had entered with the federal government years earlier in Florida.

"We had a significant motion to dismiss. This was not a futile, you know, defeatist attitude," Epstein's lawyer Martin Weinberg would tell the court later.

The huddle lasted until nearly 8:00 p.m., when Epstein was escorted back to his cell by the overnight guard Tova Noel. That would be the last time anyone outside the prison saw him alive.

2

A Corpse on 9-South

It seems to me that he outsmarted everyone so far, and his ghost is still laughing at us.

COURT STATEMENT BY ONE OF EPSTEIN'S VICTIMS

Shortly after 6:00 the next morning, the two guards on duty, Tova Noel and Michael Thomas, set out to deliver breakfast trays to the inmates on 9-South. Prison sources would later report hearing sounds of shrieking from the vicinity of Epstein's cell. Then handheld radios in the facility crackled to life, blaring the alert to all the guards on the morning shift: "Body alarm on South, body alarm on South."

Thomas said that he and Noel found the sixty-six-year-old inmate unresponsive and hanging from his bunk by a strip of orange fabric. The guard said he cut Epstein down from the makeshift noose.

"Responding [prison] staff immediately initiated life-saving measures," said the MCC warden Lamine N'Diaye in a letter to the U.S. District Court judge Richard M. Berman later that morning. They called paramedics who transported Epstein to the hospital five blocks away "for treatment of life-threatening injuries."

Epstein's cell was six feet by nine feet, according to MCC employees we interviewed, about half the size of an average parking space. The floor was dark gray concrete. A bunk bed, around four feet high with a metal frame, spanned the length of the far wall, and a concrete table the size of a TV dinner tray was bolted to the wall to the left of the door. This was the only furniture. Next to the entrance there was a metal toilet with no seat. The one window in the room, behind the bed, was latticed with thin wire bars.

Photos of the cell taken by investigators in the aftermath showed signs of confusion and perhaps even a struggle: one mattress on the floor, one still in place on the bottom bunk. Piles of crumpled orange sheets and fabric, a lot more than one bed's worth, were strewn around the room. A discarded sleep apnea machine was next to the toilet, with an upended paper coffee cup tossed on top of the wires. Nearby, there appeared to be a couple of brown puddles—or stains—on the concrete floor.

After Epstein's death, investigators found a yellow legal pad on the table with a few lines scribbled on it in ballpoint pen:[1]

> [Guard] kept me in a locked shower stall for one hour.
> [Guard] sent in burnt food.
> Giant bugs crawling on my hands.
> No fun!

"No fun" was underlined.

Epstein allegedly hanged himself from the frame of the upper bed bunk, about four feet high. The photos of his prison cell after his death, obtained by his brother, appear to show multiple attempts to tie nooses to different pieces of furniture. There are small scraps of orange fabric tied to the window grates, the metal frame of the bed, and even a supporting bar under the table, about half a foot off the ground.

Medicine bottles were lined up neatly on the top bunk, where the mattress had been removed. There were no drugs found in Epstein's system during the toxicology report, and Dr. Michael Baden, a respected independent pathologist who observed Epstein's autopsy on behalf of his family members, said the bottles contained over-the-counter pills.

Epstein was six feet tall, nearly two feet taller than the height of the bunk bed. To hang himself from it, prison insiders said, he would have had to lean forward and possibly kneel, to cut off his circulation, until he suffocated.

"For him to pull the sheet tight, that means he would have had to go to the bottom bunk, tie the sheet through the wiring that's holding the top bunk, put it around his neck, and somehow try to lean forward, or something like this, to apply the pressure to cut off his circulation," Albie Rivera, a former MCC correctional lieutenant who worked at the prison for more than a decade, told us.

Epstein, strapped to a gurney and still clad in an orange jumpsuit, was wheeled into New York-Presbyterian Lower Manhattan Hospital around 7:30 a.m. A paramedic worked a manual breathing tube into his mouth, but resuscitation efforts were no use by then. He was pronounced dead at 7:47 a.m., although a subsequent autopsy would indicate he was deceased long before he arrived.

Dr. Michael Baden, the pathologist hired by Epstein's lawyers to monitor the autopsy, told us that the financier had been dead for at least forty-five minutes, but more likely for hours, before the two guards reported finding him and started initiating "life-saving measures."

———

As news spread that Saturday morning, reactions were varied and emotions mixed.

Moneymen, political players, socialites, and media moguls waking up on the Upper East Side—the few who hadn't yet made it out to the Hamptons—must have breathed a sigh of relief. In some ways, the deceased could be said to be "in" elite Manhattan circles but not "of" them. Perhaps, at the same time, he reflected the true nature of his world—their world—in ways they would never admit, even to themselves. At any rate, he was gone, and whatever secrets he had held were safe.

Others reacted with outrage. Gloria Allred, the celebrity attorney representing several of Epstein's underage victims, was home at her beachfront condo in Malibu on August 10 when she first got word that Epstein was dead. She scrambled to contact her clients so that she could break the news to them before they heard it on TV or, worse, from an inquiring reporter.

"It was, of course, surprising and shocking," recalled Allred in an interview. "I had no reason to believe that this would happen. Could happen. Never entered my mind."

"I was concerned about [my clients] because, naturally, there would be the questions that everybody has: How could this have happened? Why did it happen?"

Allred had plenty of questions about Epstein's death. How could such a high-value inmate, who had reportedly attempted suicide just three weeks before, have had the means and opportunity to kill himself? Wasn't he supposed to be on suicide watch?

"I felt that the system had failed the victims for many years in

Florida, and elsewhere, and now the system failed them again," she said when reached on the phone. "It's failed Epstein, and it's failed the court."

Epstein's legal team was even more shocked.

In the days before his death, "we did not see a despairing, despondent suicidal person," one of his attorneys, Martin Weinberg, told U.S. District Court judge Richard M. Berman days later.[2]

Weinberg noted that Epstein had been preparing to file a bail appeal motion on Monday, August 12. "The timing for a pretrial detainee to commit suicide on August 10, when his bail pending appeal motion is being filed on August 12, strikes us as implausible," he said.

"We're not here without significant doubts regarding the conclusion of suicide," said Weinberg. "We are not here to say what happened. We don't know what happened. But we deeply want to know what happened to our client."

Finding information, even for Epstein's lawyers and family members, would prove difficult. The self-proclaimed financier's cellmate had been transferred the morning before he died, and he had not been replaced, despite directives from prison psychologists that Epstein not be housed alone.

MCC officials also neglected to preserve the scene where the body was found. Thomas, the prison guard on duty, claimed he cut down Epstein's body from a noose, making it difficult for investigators to determine what position he died in. Prison officials had also called paramedics to transport his body to a hospital, instead of keeping the body in place, as they are required to do in the case of an inmate death.

By the time the Department of Justice investigators arrived, a parade of correctional officers, prison staff, and paramedics had already walked through Epstein's cell, potentially disrupting or contaminating the scene. The prison also immediately transferred the other inmates in Epstein's tier to other locations in the prison, making it more difficult to locate witnesses.

"Instead of having the cell in the condition it was found, if he had been dead for 45 minutes or two hours or four hours, there were efforts to move him and, therefore, make it more difficult to reconstruct whether or not he died of suicide or some other cause," Weinberg told the court.

If Epstein had indeed killed himself, that should be clear in the autopsy required by New York state law. However, if something fishy happened, it seemed not impossible that the government report would be untrustworthy.

One of Epstein's attorneys had a connection with Dr. Baden, and persuaded Epstein's brother, Mark, to hire Baden to independently observe the autopsy.

Baden is perhaps the most well-known forensic pathologist in the country and host of HBO's documentary series *Autopsy*. Baden, eighty-five, a grandfatherly man with a white mustache, was the former chief medical examiner of New York City and has conducted more than twenty thousand autopsies over his career. He is famous—or as famous as a pathologist can be—but he also is well respected in the medical community. A rare breed.

The autopsy was conducted the day after Epstein's death by Dr. Kristin Roman, fifty-four, a respected veteran with the city's Medical Examiner's Office. "The beautiful thing about the body is that it doesn't lie," she once told a reporter. "It tells you its story."[3]

As the two pathologists examined Epstein's body, the first thing that caught Baden's eye was the unusual location of the ligature mark.

It was right in the middle of Epstein's neck, a thin, dark red line running horizontally across the Adam's apple.

"The ligature mark on the neck was lower than in the usual suicidal hanging. Usually the ligature is high up near the mandible, the jawbone. And here it was in the middle of the neck, which is more common in homicidal strangulation," Baden revealed over the course of a series of interviews.

The doctors also noticed there was no sign in the legs of a purplish marbling effect—known as lividity—that is typically seen when blood settles in the lower extremities after death.

"The lividity and settling of the blood is normally on the lowest part of the body," said Baden. "If he dies hanging, upright hanging, the lividity is both front and back on the legs, because that's where the blood settles. And in this instance there was no such lividity present, so it didn't look like a normal, traditional hanging."

When the pathologists looked under the skin, they found something else—an anomaly that Baden said he had not seen before in his sixty-year career.

There were three separate fractures in the front of Epstein's neck: the left and right cartilage (also known as the Adam's apple), and a horseshoe-shaped bone under the chin called the hyoid.

In the early 1970s, Baden was appointed by Governor Nelson Rockefeller to sit on a medical review board that examines every death that takes place in the New York state and city prison systems. He continues to sit on the board to this day.

According to Baden, nearly 90 percent of the thousand suicidal prison hangings he has reviewed include no fractures. Around 10 percent have a fractured hyoid, and in rare cases he has seen a fracture of the cartilage.

"We've never had three fractures," said Baden. "We haven't seen that, that I can recall, in almost fifty years we've examined every single case."

Baden said these injuries are far more common in strangulation murders.

"We've had multiple fractures if there's been a manual strangulation or ligature strangulation, where the loop, the rope, or the hands go across the Adam's apple, the thyroid cartilage," he said.

According to Roman's notes, which were obtained by Epstein's brother, Mark, the body also had bruising on the back of the neck and an injection mark on the inner arm. There were also burst capillaries in Epstein's eyes, which Baden claimed were more consistent with manual strangulation, which can build up pressure in the face.

Baden said the bruising could have been caused by an Emergency Medical Technician placing a brace around Epstein's neck. He said the injection mark was fresh and could have come from attempts by paramedics to revive Epstein, but he said federal officials have declined to say whether paramedics injected him with anything.

The findings were enough to raise questions. At the conclusion of the autopsy, Roman said she needed more information to determine the cause and manner of death. She issued a temporary death certificate, indicating that the autopsy was "inconclusive."

3
Stonewalling

n the wake of the autopsy report, social media theories flourished. Epstein was killed by the Mossad, claimed YouTube commentators and anti-Semitic bloggers. He was assassinated by the Clintons or Donald Trump, claimed Republicans and Democrats depending on their partisan affiliation. He was still alive and living it up on an island—maybe extracted from the prison in a CIA operation—and the dead body was a fake or a double.

The Office of Chief Medical Examiner in New York City, perhaps realizing the exploding PR crisis, took quick action in an attempt to quash the theories. Five days after issuing a temporary death certificate and labeling the cause "inconclusive," New York City's chief medical examiner, Barbara Sampson, announced that she would be changing the manner of death to "suicide."

What had prompted that change in just a few days? Sampson declined to give specifics, saying that the determination was made "after careful review of all investigative information, including complete autopsy findings." But the announcement came only amid immense public pressure and withering media scrutiny into the story.

In spite of public skepticism, there was certainly evidence to support the conclusion that Epstein took his own life. Suicides are not uncommon in prisons. He had revised his will just a couple of days before his death. He had, by the prison's determination, attempted suicide just weeks before (although he had denied it to friends and lawyers). He was also accustomed to an extremely comfortable lifestyle and was disgusted with his new living conditions behind bars.

"Mental abuse for a man that lived one of the best lifestyles in the world would have crushed him. He didn't have the inner strength . . . few people would," said Epstein's former boss in the investment banking industry Steven Hoffenberg, who himself spent eighteen years in prison for financial fraud, including a stint at the Metropolitan Correctional Center.

Epstein's former lawyer Alan Dershowitz said he believes Epstein was distraught at the possibility of spending the rest of his life in jail.

"I think he didn't see the light at the end of the tunnel, and he thought he was going to spend the rest of his life in prison, and that was not something he would want to do," said Dershowitz. "I haven't seen the [medical] evidence, and I have an open mind about everything, but I think the likelihood is that he took his own life because he didn't want to spend the rest of his life in prison and didn't see any exit route."

Lending further evidence to the suicide theory was the earlier alleged attempt, in July. In that case, Epstein was found unconscious in his cell with pieces of fabric around his neck, according to Department of Justice officials. The responding guards reportedly dropped the unconscious Epstein on his face twice while carrying him out of the cell, one inmate told the podcast *Epstein: Devil in the Darkness*.[1]

"When they carried him out of the cell, man, they dropped him on his face. Face-first. I heard it hit the floor with the loudest thud. I'll never forget it because it was sickening. But Epstein didn't make a sound 'cus he was out cold," said the inmate.

Prison officials determined that Epstein had attempted to commit suicide. But he denied it to his lawyers, telling them that he had some sort of clash with his bunkmate, the accused quadruple murderer and former cop Nick Tartaglione. His lawyers believed him.

"Without going into the specifics of what he said in the conversation . . . my impressions are that it was not a suicide attempt," said Epstein's lawyer David Schoen in an interview. "It wasn't an attempt to kill him, either. It was a prank gone wrong or an aggressive sort of thing from his cellmate that never should have happened."

Epstein received medical care and was placed on suicide watch. But prison psychologists took him off after just a week, although he was still required to participate in therapy sessions. He was returned to the Special Housing Unit, under doctors' orders that he be placed in the cell closest to the guards' desk so he could easily be monitored.[2] He was also assigned a new bunkmate, and his medical file prohibited prison officials from putting him in a cell by himself. But when Epstein's new cellmate was transferred out on the morning of August 9, 2019, no other inmate was transferred in.

Dr. Thomas Caffrey, the former chief psychologist at the Metropolitan Correctional Center, said in an interview that it sounded "fishy" that the prison would put "negligent officers in charge of preserving the life of a very international and high-profile inmate." He said he was surprised to learn Epstein had been removed from suicide watch after just a week.

"Someone who attempted suicide, that's very high probability of trying again, especially within the same couple of months. It sounds premature to end it after a week," Caffrey said in a phone conversation.

And yet no matter how much one could rationalize Epstein offing himself, none of those arguments should have prompted the coroner to change the official government findings.

But Sampson appears to have overruled the pathologist conducting the medical examination of the dead body—despite there apparently being no new evidence presented to call into question the findings of the exam.

"The usual information that is needed in a jail/prisoner hanging is . . . When was the person last seen, checked on? What was the position of the body when it was found? Was he dead, was he on the ground, was he hanging, was he seated?" Michael Baden said in an interview. "That's very important."

Epstein's lawyers asked Sampson for that information and were told the case was closed. Mark Epstein, Jeffrey's younger brother and his only living relative, said federal investigators have refused to provide him with medical records, names of first responders, and names of the other prisoners on Epstein's tier. The feds cited the ongoing investigation into the two prison guards who were on duty that night and first found the body, Tova Noel and Michael Thomas.

It turned out that Noel and Thomas had failed to check on Epstein for at least eight hours, despite requirements that they walk through and check on prisoners every thirty minutes. Noel, a thirty-one-year-old National Guard veteran, had been a correctional officer at MCC since 2016, a career change after brief stints at the Metropolitan Transportation Authority and as a mail handler for the U.S. Postal Service. Thomas, forty-one, was a warehouse supervisor at the prison but often moonlighted as a guard for extra cash. He had worked at MCC since 2007.

On the night and morning of Epstein's death, the guards filed "more than 75 30-minute round entries" falsely claiming that they checked on Epstein's tier, according to the DOJ.[3]

"We messed up," Thomas admitted to his supervisor after the body was found. "We didn't do any rounds."[4]

The video also showed that Noel and Thomas spent most of the night sitting at the guards' desk, which was in a common area ten to fifteen feet away from Epstein's cell, within easy earshot of his death. For two hours, the guards appeared to be sleeping at their desks. At other points of the night, they surfed the web. Noel browsed furniture sales. Thomas shopped for motorcycles. They didn't conduct any of the required checks on Epstein's tier between 10:00 p.m. and 6:00 a.m., although they did fill out logbooks claiming they made the checks. In fact, Noel, who had started working at 4:00 p.m., failed to conduct a single check during her entire time on the clock, according to the Department of Justice.

Noel was the last person to escort Epstein into his cell for the evening at 7:49. At around 10:30 p.m., she walked up to the gate outside Epstein's tier. His cell, which had a window to the tier hallway, was just a couple of feet from her. She stood outside the gate for a moment. Then she turned around and walked back to her desk.

Epstein had a history of run-ins with Noel. In notes found after his death, he accused her of serving him "burnt food." Epstein was not popular with many of the guards, who found him to be demanding and seemed annoyed by the special privileges he received—for example, the fact that he was allowed to meet with his attorneys for eight hours or more a day. The guards had to walk him back and forth to these meetings, up and down flights of stairs—more work for them.

Guards at the prison were routinely overworked due to federal budget cuts, according to Eric Young, president of the American

Federation of Government Employees Council of Prison Locals, the union for correctional officers. They often picked up double shifts, working sixteen hours or more.

"It wasn't a matter of how [suicide] happened or it happening, but it was only a matter of time for it to happen. It was inevitable. Our staff is severely overworked," Young said in a statement.[5]

At midnight, Thomas arrived for his 12:00 a.m. to 8:00 a.m. shift. He and Epstein also had something of a history. Thomas was one of the MCC guards on duty who responded to Epstein's alleged suicide attempt in July.

Prison guards have strong union protections and are rarely prosecuted for negligence, but Noel and Thomas were indicted in November on charges of falsifying records and conspiracy to defraud the government. Thomas faces a maximum of twenty years in prison; Noel faces a maximum of thirty. Noel and Thomas turned down plea agreements, according to the Associated Press.[6] Lawyers for Noel and Thomas declined to make their clients available for interviews.

Those who are familiar with the internal workings of MCC say it's hard to believe such a high-profile prisoner as Jeffrey Epstein could have died—by either suicide or otherwise—without the knowledge or assistance of prison employees.

"At nighttime like that, you can hear everything. You can hear a pin drop. Everybody's sleeping; it's quiet," Albie Rivera, the former longtime MCC guard, revealed in an interview. "If they were ten, fifteen feet away from his cell, they should have been able to hear him. You could hear him get up; you could hear everything he's doing. The window's right there, to his door, you could look. You could see what he's doing; there's no way of obstructing the view."

Would guards have been able to hear the sound of someone ripping up strips of sheets, which he allegedly used to make the nooses? "Of course," said Rivera.

"I wouldn't rule out foul play somehow," he said. "To me it sounds like he could have been killed. It's very hard to say that he killed himself."

—

There was more strangeness to come, in addition to the guards' negligence and silence. In the days after Epstein's death, news outlets reported that the surveillance camera monitoring his cell had malfunctioned the night of his death and no footage had been captured.[7]

The news sounded peculiar, even to other correctional officers who had worked at the prison.

"I find that so odd. So odd," said one former longtime guard at the Metropolitan Correctional Center in an interview. "How do you not have a functional, working camera? Of all people, that man's cell.

"Does that raise a flag in your brain? I know it does in mine," he added. "Why, in every other cell the cameras are operational, but Epstein's was not?"

Rivera said broken cameras would be quickly noticed and fixed if they were monitoring a high-value inmate.

"If there were ones that were inoperable, they should have been inoperable for only a few minutes. They would have come in and fixed them right away. Of course, especially with a high-profile inmate like that," Rivera said in an interview.

Another longtime MCC guard questioned the lack of working cameras monitoring the inside of the tier, saying this was almost unimaginable for a high-value inmate.

"There's cameras in every cell," said the correctional officer. "Now you get an individual like Epstein. Don't you think his camera should have been working? Don't you think he should have been placed in a cell that had a working, functional camera?"

There was at least one functional camera, but it was outside Epstein's tier. The footage indicated that nobody had entered or left the only door to his section the entire night, which housed eight two-man jail cells, according to the Department of Justice. However, it would not have shown the activities of any of the dozen or so inmates already on the cellblock.

It would get yet stranger months later in November 2019 when Attorney General William Barr told the Associated Press "that he personally reviewed security footage that confirmed that no one entered the area where Epstein was housed on the night he died."[8] Barr would conclude that while protocol was not followed, it was a suicide. But if he got to personally review the security footage, why were others apparently not able to see it? And, more surprisingly, why did the footage apparently disappear after his viewing? Officials would in January 2020 say the footage "no longer exists" due to "technical errors."[9]

Mark Epstein has been fighting to get more information on his brother's death, without success. "He wasn't close to his brother, but he loves his brother and he wanted to know what happened," said Dr. Baden.

Mark Epstein, a Manhattan real estate investor, said in a phone call that so far the feds have refused to provide him with medical records and the names of first responders.

The younger Epstein said he hasn't reached a conclusion on what happened to his brother. "I don't have a theory. I'm not speculating," he said. He has also been reluctant to talk to the press: "This is not about me. That's why you don't see pictures of me, I don't go on camera for anybody."

But his own review of the evidence—at least the limited number of nonpublic records he has been able to obtain—has raised questions in his mind.

Mark Epstein was able to get copies of photographs of his brother's cell and body, taken by investigators after his death. He noticed at least one strange discrepancy in the pictures: the orange noose that officials identified as the one Jeffrey Epstein used to hang himself appears to have hemmed edges and does not look as if it were cut. Mark Epstein said that seems to conflict with the account from the prison guard Michael Thomas, who said he cut the body down from the ligature.

"All we've heard from the guard is the guard said he cut him down," said Mark by phone. "If you look at the picture of the ligature . . . it was not cut and it doesn't look like it was tied to anything . . . Look at the angle of the ligature. It was a hemmed edge; it was not cut."

Autopsy photos also show dried blood on Epstein's neck surrounding the ligature mark. However, there does not appear to be blood on the noose in the photos. The discrepancy suggests that this ligature was incorrectly identified as the object used in Epstein's death.

Some have speculated that Mark Epstein could have a financial motive for questioning the suicide ruling, including a wrongful death suit against the government. Dr. Baden disputed this, insisting there is no lawsuit on the table.

"There's no money involved with this; there's no lawsuits involved in this. All that Mark wants to know is, what's the accurate cause of death and if indeed his brother committed suicide," said Baden.

Some of Epstein's close friends can't comprehend him committing suicide for a different reason. They said it would be completely out of character.

"Bullshit. He was murdered," one close friend who knew him for decades asserted in an interview. "I can't imagine that thought [of suicide] crossing his mind."

"The man could afford all the lawyers in the world. The day before that suicide, he had met with his lawyers for eight hours," said the friend. "Those lawyers were certainly giving hope for what he could do, but more importantly, he knew he could buy his way out of a lot of shit."

4
What Happened

The Possibilities

With a dead man at the Metropolitan Correctional Center and the world watching, immediately speculation grew about what actually happened that Saturday morning in August. There were only two possibilities: suicide or murder.

No theory was without holes; none would fully account for the events that took place. And, importantly, evidence was scarce. But to many who read or watched the coverage, none of that would matter. They had already made up their minds.

The official story would have the public believe that Epstein's demise was the work of his own hands. According to the chief medical examiner, he died by hanging himself. The motive was clear: after years of getting away with crimes, he realized that the jig was up. Decades in prison for a sixty-six-year-old man meant a lifetime punishment, and he did not want to face that.

"I don't care about my legacy. The minute I'm dead, I'm dead. It's over," Epstein once told a friend and adviser. "I don't care what people think of me. I only care about what's happening to me while I'm alive."

According to the suicide theory, Epstein might have died still believing that he did nothing wrong. He was keen to protest his innocence to those around him. But he was also socially and politically intelligent enough to realize that he would never be exonerated by a court of law. He therefore came to the conclusion that his tawdry ways had caught up to him and that he would never be able to escape the confines of lockup. His alleged suicide attempt weeks earlier had been his first attempt to get off easy.

Those who believe he killed himself argue that after his suicide attempt Epstein used his masterful manipulation skills to convince everyone around him that in fact he was not actually interested in taking his own life. That it had been some sort of misunderstanding with his alleged-murderer cellmate.

In this version of the story, Epstein got his way. He was alone, free to take his time to set up another suicide attempt. And this time he did it right. He quickly got his affairs in order, filing a new will two days before his death.

With a cell to himself, he was more careful this time. He fashioned the bedsheets into a noose, positioned the noose on his bed frame, and then placed it around his neck. Finally, with a drop to his knees, the noose slipped tighter and tighter around his neck, before cutting off circulation and breaking his neck, becoming the first MCC prisoner to die by suicide in thirteen years.

But that scenario did not sit well with a lot of observers. There seemed to be almost a comedy of errors that night—certainly a confluence of egregious mistakes.

Just how could the most high-value criminal defendant in America kill himself while supposedly under twenty-four-hour surveillance in federal custody? How could he have known the guards would conveniently not check on him for more than eight hours? In response to this question, another theory began to emerge—that, yes, he killed himself. But he did not act alone.

"It's hard to do," said Albie Rivera in an interview. "For him to do it that way, it would have to mean that he had this totally planned."

It's plausible he had the assistance of others. Maybe some guards or fellow inmates had helped orchestrate Epstein's final act. He needed help to get off suicide watch and return to the general prison population. He, the theory goes, used his connections within the confines of lockup to get his wishes. He needed time alone, in his own cell and without interference from prison guards. Here again, they say, he used the power at his disposal to get what he wanted.

Ever since he entered prison, he had been waving around his wealth. Just as it was a powerful elixir in the outside world, it allowed him to seduce hopeless prisoners so he could get what he wanted in the confines of MCC. This allowed him to get the space, time, and resources to do the dirty deed.

—

Some believe Epstein hanged himself but that, instead of being a suicide, it was a meticulously planned ruse by Epstein that went massively awry. An accidental death.

"He was showing he was suicidal to get moved to a hospital," said Laura Goldman, a friend of Epstein's longtime girlfriend and alleged accomplice, Ghislaine Maxwell, in an interview.

"And why do I know that? Because I was there and that's how I got out."

Goldman spent time at MCC in the 1990s after threatening a man who she claimed sexually assaulted her. She said she was able to get transferred to a mental health facility after an unsuccessful suicide attempt.

After she learned that Epstein was locked up at MCC in July 2019, Goldman said she talked to Ghislaine's sister Isabel about the incident.

"I did mention when he was arrested, 'You know that's where I was, and I attempted suicide,'" said Goldman. "Ghislaine and Isabel both knew that."

Epstein's first alleged suicide attempt in July had gotten him placed on twenty-four-hour suicide watch, but it hadn't gotten him a transfer out of MCC, nor out of the notoriously dilapidated Special Housing Unit. Epstein would not have been a candidate for the facility's general population because his safety would be at risk as such a high-profile prisoner accused of underage sex crimes.

Epstein, a gifted manipulator, successfully persuaded MCC psychologists to take him off suicide watch after just a week. Would a second, botched attempt have shown that the prison couldn't properly supervise him and be entrusted with his protection? Would his lawyers, the victims, and the public demand that he be transferred somewhere that could adequately ensure his safety?

One of Epstein's lawyers, Martin Weinberg, tore into the conditions at MCC during a court hearing shortly after his client's death.

"We think your Honor trusted the government, the Bureau of Prisons, to keep our client safe and keep him in civilized conditions," said Weinberg. "I've called [MCC] medieval. There's vermin on the floor. There is wet from the plumbing. There is no sunlight. There is limited exercise. It is simply conditions that no pretrial detainee—and I would go farther as a criminal defense lawyer—no United States defendant should be subjected to."

Epstein's own list of grievances against the prison—the burned food, the bugs—were laid out in the legal pad left in plain sight on his cell table. Photos of his room after his death show that the top mattress from his bunk had been pulled onto the floor, where it was placed perpendicular to the bottom bunk. Why? Would it have been uncomfortable for him to rest his knees on the concrete floor while kneeling forward into the noose?

Dr. Baden, the defense pathologist, estimated that Epstein died several hours before the guards reportedly found him at 6:30 a.m. Was Epstein expecting them to check on him during their mandatory 3:00 a.m. head count—the one they allegedly slept through?

As someone familiar with the prison, Goldman thinks it's a serious possibility.

"Listen, it was a reasonable gambit, except for the fact they didn't come and check on him, that had he attempted suicide twice, he either would have been moved to [a hospital], or Oklahoma where there's a male mental health facility," she said. "But his lawyers might have been able to get him out of that because they would have said they need him to help prepare for trial."

—

It might be possible to explain away the failure of the cameras and guards as neglect. But it's also possible that there was collusion, not for assisted suicide, but for someone to take out Epstein without his knowledge or consent. Or, as this theory is popularly known, "Epstein didn't kill himself."

This was another alluring possibility. It made sense. Epstein had tales to tell about some of the richest, most powerful men in the world. And contrary to public speculation, those around him thought he was optimistic about his chances to get out of prison.

"So the guy killed himself the next day, but on Friday he's planning on fighting this case and he's all pumped up about it?" his lawyer David Schoen said with some measure of disbelief during an interview.

"I don't buy into those conspiracy theories. I don't think Bill Clinton killed him or Hillary," he said.

But Schoen does not believe that Epstein just up and offed himself, either. "I think it was just a regular, old somebody [who] killed him," Schoen said at his Atlanta-area home. This meant a fellow inmate, rather than a politician who might have been compromised. In this theory, the deed was done by someone who did not want Epstein alive, but not necessarily for anything that had occurred outside MCC walls.

"It would be that somehow a prison door is left open, is left unlocked. [Epstein's] door and another prisoner's door will be left unlocked," said Baden. "And that prisoner can go in and do what he wants and come back out and nobody would be the wiser.

"But it would require somebody to be active in it. One person would have to do that," Baden added.

MCC guards said cell doors are not locked electronically at the prison. Officers still carry old-fashioned Folger Adam keys that open the tier gates and the individual cell doors. Rivera revealed that it was possible certain cells could be "purposely unlocked and left unlocked" by a correctional officer or someone else with a key.

"Whoever those two officers were, if they allowed somebody else to go in and do that to him. That's possible," said Rivera.

"I honestly believe, if that did happen, it would have had to happen with the help of some of the staff. It's almost impossible for somebody to plan that, or be able to get it off without help. You got to have some type of help."

This wasn't the first mysterious death in this jail. On May 19, 2015, a prisoner at MCC named Roberto Grant died in custody while awaiting sentencing on robbery charges. Prison officials initially told Grant's family that the thirty-five-year-old had died of a drug overdose while high on synthetic marijuana.[1]

"He showed signs of being choked," said Andrew Laufer, an attorney for Grant, in an interview. "His mother and his ex-wife came down to the prison to find out what happened. They told them it was an OD on K2, which it wasn't."

The autopsy found no drugs in his system. But it did find signs of "blunt force trauma," including signs of strangulation and injury to the hyoid bone in his neck. Still, the manner of death was ruled "inconclusive" by the New York City Medical Examiner's Office.

Like Epstein's case, there was no surveillance footage available from Grant's cell on the night of his death, said Laufer. Grant had also had bad relationships with some of the correctional officers, according to his lawyer. But his family, who sued MCC for $20 million, believes he was murdered, by either other inmates or guards, and his cause of death was covered up by prison officials.

"I think [the prison has] been preventing us from finding out more information. I believe that they want to do anything but take responsibility for my client's murder," said Laufer. "And that goes for any other case I've had. I've had clients lose fingers in doorways—get chopped off. I've had clients get fractures. They never want to admit any wrongdoing. It's always the client's fault, as they always like to allege."

Laufer said he sees some similarities between the deaths of his client and Epstein. But in Epstein's case, he said he wouldn't rule out negligence by the guards.

"My personal feeling, and until I see the additional evidence, is gross negligence. I see plenty of that there," he said.

Alan Dershowitz, who was still in regular contact with Epstein's legal team at the time of his death, said Epstein's attorneys seemed to have a fairly strong case and were confident of their chances.

"The thing that does surprise me is he was more of an optimist," said Dershowitz. "He had a pretty good case. His lawyers told me he had a shot at winning. That's why his lawyers don't believe he killed himself."

Others, including the president of the United States and other politicians, openly suggested that Epstein's death was somehow the result of foul play.[2]

"I can understand people who immediately, whose minds went to sort of the worst-case scenario because it was a perfect storm of screw-ups," Attorney General Bill Barr admitted in an interview.[3] "I think it was important to have a roommate in there with him and we're looking into why that wasn't done, and I think every indication is that was a screw-up," Barr told the Associated Press. "The systems to assure that was done were not followed."

The seemingly wild theories about Epstein's death were not without some shred of scientific evidence. Dr. Baden took to Fox News to contradict the official narrative one morning in October 2019.

"I think that the evidence points toward homicide rather than suicide," he told the cable news channel.[4]

Explaining the specific injuries suffered by Epstein that morning in his cell, Baden stated that they were "more consistent with ligature homicidal strangulation" than suicide. "Hanging does not cause these broken bones and homicide does," he said. "A huge amount of pressure was applied."

Baden's explosive findings were, for the record, rejected by New York City officials. "Our investigation concluded that the cause of Mr. Epstein's death was hanging and the manner of death was suicide. We stand by that determination," Sampson said in a statement to Fox News.[5] "We continue to share information around the medical investigation with Mr. Epstein's family, their representatives, and their pathology consultant."

But if, as the meme succinctly suggests, the government is hiding something and "Epstein didn't kill himself," then who killed him? It is incontrovertible that quite a few stood to gain by his death. The rich and famous, with much to lose, certainly feared that Epstein would sing to authorities. Rumors swirled that he had blackmail—videos, photos. By contrast, very few people, if any, benefited by having so many questions unanswered when Epstein died.

There was another factor that led to the belief becoming so widespread. Epstein had gotten away with his crimes for so long, with hardly anyone paying any sort of price. Additionally, media and institutions had helped provide cover for him to operate with impunity. The idea that now, all of a sudden, the media could be trusted to tell the truth about Epstein after getting him so wrong for so many years belied belief for many around the country.

Even after details of Epstein's depraved crimes started to go public, his mysterious hold over some of the world's most powerful men continued. He and Prince Andrew strolled together through Central Park, in full view of photographers, months after Epstein was released from house arrest for soliciting underage prostitutes. He also hosted the former Treasury secretary Larry Summers at his office and flew Bill Gates to Palm Beach on his Gulfstream jet. He dined with Katie Couric, George Stephanopoulos, Chelsea Handler, and Woody Allen at his twenty-one-thousand-square-foot Manhattan mansion.

These were just some of the big names caught up in a story driven by fraud, theft, and rape. Epstein's death exposed at least some of the dirty secrets of how wealth, politics, celebrity, and the media enabled this predator to harm countless victims over the course of decades. And what other secrets might there be that would drive someone to drastic action in order to keep them hidden?

Which is why most who knew Epstein, whether they liked him, were violated by him, or simply had a business relationship with him, believe he was murdered.

—

While there are a number of ways that Epstein's murder in MCC could have been carried out, that still leaves wide open the question of *who* did it, or ordered it done. Given Epstein's decades of sordid behavior and the many influential figures who crossed his path as it was going on, the list gets long fast. But the picture will become clearer after a look back at Epstein's life, how he treated those he met along the way, and how key figures in politics, the media, and the intellectual elite still fear telling the truth about Jeffrey Epstein.

5
Blackmail

Guests approaching Epstein's home on the Upper East Side saw a sedate and gorgeous building with views of the Frick Collection, located across the street. They entered through fifteen-foot oak doors that emphasized the grandeur of this desirable New York address.

The first thing they would see upon entering would give them quite a shock: an oil portrait of President Bill Clinton, wearing a blue dress and red high heels, sitting seductively in a chair in the Oval Office.

"It was hanging up there prominently—as soon as you walked in—in a room to the right," the *New York Post* quoted a source as saying.[1] "Everybody who saw it laughed and smirked."

The painting, titled *Parsing Bill*, created by the artist Petrina Ryan-Kleid in 2012 and sold at Tribeca Ball, an arts school fund-raiser, is obviously a tongue-in-cheek mockery of Clinton's most embarrassing and devastating moment as president—his Oval Office affair with a then intern who famously kept a semen-stained blue dress as evidence of her affair with the commander in chief.

Beyond the sick joke, the message of the Clinton portrait seemed obvious: a warning to his rich and powerful guests that he had dirt on them, and that they had better do as he asked. Epstein was friendly with Clinton, proudly displaying this visual message to all his acquaintances. And he did not hesitate in his final years to explain to others that this was one way he maintained power.

On August 16, 2018, Epstein invited a *New York Times* journalist to that very home to help spread the word.

"The overriding impression I took away from our roughly 90-minute conversation was that Mr. Epstein knew an astonishing number of rich, famous and powerful people, and had photos to prove it. He also claimed to know a great deal about these people, some of it potentially damaging or embarrassing, including details about their supposed sexual proclivities and recreational drug use," the journalist James B. Stewart would report.[2]

Stewart added, "During our conversation, Mr. Epstein made no secret of his own scandalous past—he'd pleaded guilty to state charges of soliciting prostitution from underage girls and was a registered sex offender—and acknowledged to me that he was a pariah in polite society. At the same time, he seemed unapologetic. His very notoriety, he said, was what made so many people willing to confide in him. Everyone, he suggested, has secrets and, he added, compared with his own, they seemed innocuous. People confided in him without feeling awkward or embarrassed, he claimed."

The tell-all article was written after Epstein's death, because the conversation occurred under an on-background agreement, which the writer asserted lapsed upon his interlocutor's demise. (An agreement to keep comments on background is a condition that usually allows the reporter to use information learned from a source, and usually even quotations, as long as the source himself is never specifically identified.)

And yet the conversation, as retold by Stewart, offers one of the clearest views into Epstein's mind.

———

In 1995, a twenty-six-year-old by the name of Maria Farmer had recently taken up a job at Epstein's New York mansion. Her job was to work the front desk.

She noticed suspicious activity. "I saw many, many, many, many, many" young women coming to the house, she recalled in a 2019 interview with CBS.[3]

"All day long. I saw Ghislaine going to get the women. She went to places like Central Park. I was with her a couple of times in the car . . . She would say, 'Stop the car.' And she would dash out and get a child."

Farmer recalls that Ghislaine Maxwell, Epstein's alleged procurer, told her she was "getting Victoria's Secret models."

Farmer was unsettled. "One day I said to Jeffrey, 'What goes on in this house?' Like, 'Why are you always upstairs?' And he said, 'I'll show you.' And so he took me up there in the elevator. And we went—he showed me all of Ghislaine's quarters."

In his own bathroom, Epstein had on display "a marble, like, altar thing over here, and he said that's where he gets his massages."

He also showed her the intricate camera system he had set up throughout the house. "I looked on the cameras, and I saw toilet, toilet, bed, bed, toilet, bed. I'm like 'I am never going to use the restroom here, and I'm never going to sleep here,'" she told the news network.

Epstein told her that the video footage from his house was meticulously stored and safeguarded. "I keep it. I keep everything in my safe," he told her.

Why, exactly, he chose to disclose his high-tech surveillance system to his employ is a matter of speculation. Perhaps Epstein wanted those he sought to overpower to know that he had dirt on them too. Regardless, Farmer would not be the only one to hear his boasts.

One close friend said he asked Epstein to give his wife a tour of his home in New York a few years ago. During the visit, Epstein proudly boasted about the cameras he had in each room.

"He gave [my wife and I] a tour. And all he kept pointing out was cameras. There were cameras everywhere," said the friend in an interview.

"He had cameras in every room of his house. He had cameras in the bathroom. He was doing it for some reason. He didn't tell me what the reason was, but here's a good guess: there's a lot of famous people he had something on.

"That was the first time I heard him tell [about] the cameras, the cameras, the cameras. I kind of knew that was what was going on, and he'd allude to it in other ways, but at this point he was proud of it."

The greatest evidence of Epstein's photo cache was discovered in a raid on his New York mansion shortly after his July 6, 2019, arrest at Teterboro Airport in New Jersey.

Prosecutors said they recovered what amounted to child pornography, nude snaps of his victims. "At least hundreds—and perhaps thousands—of sexually suggestive photographs of fully- or partially nude females" were found safely stored at Epstein's home,[4] according to a court memo written by the U.S. attorney for the Southern District of New York, Geoffrey Berman, on July 8, 2019.

The images "appear to be of underage girls, including at least one girl who, according to her counsel, was underage at the time the relevant photographs were taken," the prosecutor stated.

More surprising, perhaps, was how neatly organized the stash appeared at his home. It was laid out in "compact discs with hand-written labels including the following: 'Young [Name] + [Name],' 'Misc nudes 1,' and 'Girl pics nude,'" the documents would allege.

Although it is not known if the images featuring child porn also featured Epstein or others in his orbit, he proudly kept an array of G-rated photos of his high-profile friends on display for any common visitor.

Epstein showed off his photos with world leaders, pointing to a framed picture of the crown prince of Saudi Arabia, Mohammed bin Salman, and saying, "That's M.B.S." The journalist James B. Stewart took note of photos of Woody Allen, a good friend of Epstein's who has also been accused of sexual misconduct, and Bill Clinton, another friend who likewise has been accused of sexual assault and even rape.

But while it has become clear just *how* Epstein went about obsessively documenting the visits of the rich and powerful to his home and their private activities while there—he was hardly shy about the camera system even when he was alive—his motivation for doing so is less obvious. *Why* did Epstein feel the need to rig his bedrooms and bathrooms with cameras? Was it just his own voyeuristic perversion? Or was there something deeper?

Arguably, this obsession with following and filming and documenting the most intimate habits of the powerful came out of Epstein's obsession with power itself. It wasn't just the sexual behavior of his powerful friends that interested him; it was everything about their lives. This might have been used for blackmail and other purposes to Epstein's direct advantage, but his fascination went deeper than that. He had conned his way into the upper ranks of high society but perhaps still felt a bit like the outsider looking in. Today we might call that impostor syndrome. He was around people with real power, but he had to find different ways to try to grasp it for himself. And to understand the real roots of that obsession, you have to understand where he came from.

PART II
An Indecent Life

6

Ill-Gotten Gains

Years of Deception and Fraudulent Fortunes

He could see your weaknesses.

STEVEN HOFFENBERG

A photo in Epstein's senior yearbook shows him at sixteen years old, walking shirtless along the beach in Coney Island. He's chubby and pale, his belly hanging over the top of a pair of old jeans cut into knee-length swim shorts. His frizzy brown hair is badly in need of a trim. His eyes are trained on the ground, an awkward gummy smile on his face.

The man who would one day wield so much power and wealth, inflicting so much pain on poor suffering victims along the way, in high school was poor, unattractive, and unhappy with that state of affairs.

"He was getting beaten up all the time for being a schmuck—looking like a schmuck, or whatever. He must have had a rough time, and there was probably never a girl that ever looked at him," said one longtime friend of Epstein's in an interview.

"He really had some kind of contempt for women . . . And I think he was getting back at all those fifteen-year-old, sixteen-year-old girls who would never talk to him because he looked like such a schmuck," added the friend.

He had a rough time, and it seemed that he decided to do whatever it would take to leave it behind, to learn charm in order to manipulate those in power, and to get what he wanted from men, women—and girls.

Epstein was born January 20, 1953, the day President Dwight D. Eisenhower was inaugurated. The elder son of Seymour and Pauline, the lucky few from their respective families who had not perished in the Holocaust, Jeffrey Epstein grew up in a middle-class area of Coney Island, nearly an hour away from Manhattan using public transportation. The neighborhood was Sea Gate, the oldest gated community in the city.[1]

The Epsteins were rare in that both Seymour and Pauline worked but were still firmly on the very lower end of middle class. Seymour, born December 4, 1916, in Manhattan to European immigrant parents, first held down construction work, where he demolished homes, before getting a more stable job with New York City's Parks Department, where he picked up trash. Neighbors have recalled Seymour's stutter. Pauline, born October 5, 1918, in Brooklyn to Lithuanian immigrant parents, worked as an aide in a school.

The Epsteins lived in an apartment taking up the middle third of a decently sized house in Sea Gate at Maple Avenue. In 1955, Mark Epstein was born, stretching the family's already thin resources. The family couldn't afford much more than the essentials.

"[Jeffrey] hated his childhood because they were poor," recalled Steven Hoffenberg in an interview.

Poor though he was, Epstein had one notable resource. By all accounts, he was smart. A natural math whiz who skipped a couple grades. A piano virtuoso. He was also generous, mentoring other kids at Lafayette High School along the way.

Despite being remembered as a schmuck, Epstein seems to have had at least a bit of a social life. His friends affectionately called him Eppy, and he had at least one girlfriend, who remembered him fondly years later.

"That last year in school, I think he kind of loved me," one high school sweetheart recalled in the book *Filthy Rich*. "One night on the beach he kissed me. In fact, our history teacher made up a mock wedding invitation for Jeffrey and myself to show to the class. That seems pretty inappropriate now. But back then, we all thought it was funny. Jews and the Italians, that was pretty much who went to Lafayette High School. They didn't socialize that much. And though my mother was crazy about him, she told me Jewish boys don't marry Italians."[2]

Epstein graduated early and quickly moved to leave Coney Island behind. In the fall of 1969, he enrolled at the Cooper Union and studied physics. The college's main attracting feature for the student from humble roots was its cost—free. He was sixteen years old, but as he did in high school, he began tutoring his fellow students. This time he charged for his services. For the first time, Jeffrey Epstein was a working man.

Mysteriously, Epstein, despite his brilliance, did not seem able to stick to his studies. He lasted only until the spring of 1971, before he left without earning a degree. Months later he began studying mathematics at New York University. He was affiliated with the prestigious Courant Institute of Mathematical Sciences. He would leave that higher institution in June 1974, though it is unclear why, again without any sort of degree.

Somewhere along the way he found other work—an unceremonious job in Brooklyn as a roofer. It seemed the boy from the poor family was going back to where he came from.

But Epstein would not tolerate returning to his old world. And it is at this point that he would begin to try his hand at being a confidence man—reliant on the world of fraud, distortion, and lying to get ahead.

His first documented fraud was fudging his résumé to get a job at the Dalton School. Founded in 1919, Dalton is one of the most prestigious educational institutions in New York City and normally hired only the best. Yet somehow, in the early 1970s, the college dropout and former roofer Jeffrey Epstein persuaded them to hire him to teach the children of Manhattan's leading families.

He is believed to have been hired by the school's headmaster, who coincidentally left the school amid an unrelated brouhaha months before Epstein's official start date in 1974. The schoolmaster was Donald Barr, the father of William Barr, who would serve as attorney general of the United States at the time of Epstein's arrest and subsequent death.[3]

At Dalton, Epstein taught physics and math, and he coached the school's math team. His students were mostly the older kids, high school upperclassmen who were seventeen or eighteen years old, not too far off from Epstein himself, who was only in his early twenties.

For a working-class kid, this was a glimpse into a whole new world. True, he was only a lowly teacher, but his students were the kids of the adults who ran the city—the political players, the media honchos, and the money managers.

"I come from a background where I had no money and it was only by understanding math and science that I was able to live the life I currently lead," Epstein would later recount in court documents.

Or, as his former boss Hoffenberg described it in an interview, "His greatest dream was to be superrich, to be a multimillionaire, generated by this hatred of his childhood."

At Dalton, Epstein socialized with his students and was well liked by them, though in retrospect some worrisome traits began to emerge. Specifically, it was the way he interacted with young female students. "It was just kind of a general circle of girls," the former student Scott Spizer recalled in an interview with National Public Radio. "He was much more present amongst the students, specifically the girl students, during nonteaching hours . . . it seemed just, it was kind of inappropriate."

There was an acute awareness of what Kerry Lawrence of the graduating class of 1976 calls "creepiness."[4]

"When you had a faculty member that girls were paying attention to, it was somewhat disconcerting," Lawrence added.

Years later, Epstein would demure in a deposition on whether he had sexual relations with any students. Asked whether he had been intimate with anyone he taught, he answered, "Not that I remember," a typical lawyerly response that left open the possibility of such teacher-student relations.

After two years at Dalton, the school decided to move on from the unconventional teacher because he wasn't "up to snuff," the interim headmaster Peter Branch would recall many decades later. "It was determined that he had not adequately grown as a new teacher to the standard of the school," he would tell another reporter.[5]

Which of course was always true. Epstein had no business being a teacher, because he did not have the qualifications required to serve in such a capacity. He had weaseled his way into the job, only to be found out eventually that he did not have the qualifications. An important lesson, perhaps, in retrospect—that the longer the con, the harder and harder it is to maintain.

For his next opportunity, Epstein seems to have switched tactics a bit, attaining it not exactly by lying but by using charm to get what he wanted from the powerful people with whom he surrounded himself. Either because he knew his end was near or because it was all part of his plan, Epstein used parent-teacher conferences to network, telling his kids' parents that he was looking for work on Wall Street, according to the *Miami Herald*.[6]

According to *Filthy Rich*, Epstein began tutoring the son of the Bear Stearns executive Alan "Ace" Greenberg, and some believed he dated his daughter, Lynne.[7] Then he charmed the father into giving him a job at the prestigious investment bank. The college dropout from Brooklyn scored a job on Wall Street in 1976, at a time when most hires there were graduates from the most prestigious colleges in America.

Epstein thrived. He picked up the language, innately understood financial concepts, and finally began to make decent—and soon great—money. He also, for apparently the first time, got his taste of forbidden fruits, entering an inappropriate relationship with his assistant.

But that would not be enough. And soon he was unsatisfied and looking for love. Epstein was highlighted as "Bachelor of the Month" in the July 1980 issue of *Cosmopolitan* magazine.[8]

Accompanied by a photo of the Wall Streeter sporting his best impression of a Beatles haircut, the personal ad stated, "Financial strategist Jeffrey Epstein, 27, talks only to people who make over a million a year! If you're 'a cute Texas girl,' write this New York dynamo at 55 Water St., 49th floor, N.Y.C. 10041."

The Brooklyn boy had created a new persona: a "New York dynamo" who works only with the most wealthy and who cultivated exotic—southern!—women.

Thanks perhaps to the effect of his alter ego, Epstein quickly moved up the chain. That same summer, he was named a limited partner, a step below full partner but still a remarkable rise for someone with no family connections and no financial experience. He had only his relationship with Greenberg and a quickly developed mentor-mentee relationship with Bear Stearns's CEO, James Cayne.

A year later, under murky circumstances and more than a whiff of scandal, he was out. There were allegations of an inappropriate and perhaps illegal loan, insider trading, and a deal gone bad. But none of the charges stuck. Asked by SEC investigators about the rumors of his departure in testimony given on April 1, 1981, Epstein admitted that he heard "it was having to do with an illicit affair with a secretary." It is unclear whether Epstein himself believed whether the rumor mill had gotten this one correct.

Epstein also told SEC investigators "he was offended by the company's investigation of a twenty-thousand-dollar loan he'd made to his friend Warren Eisenstein," according to *Filthy Rich*. "On top of that, questions about Epstein's expenses had come up. In the end, Bear Stearns fined him $2,500—an embarrassing thing, to be sure."[9]

Scandal could not keep Epstein down, however. He struck out on his own, in a solo venture he registered to his apartment and called the Intercontinental Assets Group Inc. He intended the company to specialize in recovering assets for the ultra-wealthy, and soon enough he was a successful "financial bounty hunter"—a moniker he clearly relished.

Epstein also started offering "strategic advice" that would assist his clients in limiting their tax liability. He counted on the fact that wealthy clients would spend millions of dollars for his services if they stood to save tens or hundreds of millions in taxes. By the late 1980s, he changed his business plan again, setting up shop under the name J. Epstein & Company. His private firm's gimmick would be to manage the money for the richest of the rich: billionaires.

Shortly after beginning his new firm, Epstein found two anchor clients. The first was the client of a lifetime, the underwear magnate Leslie H. Wexner, the chairman and CEO of L Brands, which owns the clothing company the Limited and the lingerie maker Victoria's Secret.

They met in a strange and purely accidental way when Epstein was seated next to Wexner's friend Robert Meister on a flight to Palm Beach. Both were in first class. Meister, an insurance executive, talked up his client Wexner, who he revealed was unhappy with his money managers. Epstein's services as a money manager were offered, and soon thereafter an introduction was made.

The two hit it off. Wexner and Epstein were fast friends and even closer business associates. "People have said it's like we have one brain between the two of us: each has a side," Epstein told the *Vanity Fair* profiler Vicky Ward in a breakout piece about him in 2003 titled "The Talented Mr. Epstein."[10]

Wexner's trust in Epstein was so immense he'd end up signing over his house—the Manhattan mansion considered the largest residential home in the city—to him. Epstein would be named a board member of his personal foundation. But perhaps the biggest sign of his trust was giving him power of attorney over his wealth, allowing the young, and perhaps somewhat unproven, wealth manager to have the financial power of a billionaire.

Epstein helped design and manage the building of Wexner's yacht,

Limitless. He involved himself in all matters business and personal, often visiting the clothing tycoon's Columbus, Ohio, mansion. It helped that Epstein eventually acquired his own home nearby in New Albany, Ohio.

Epstein even helped the Wexners find a nanny. "I'll just put Jeffrey on it," Abigail Wexner, Les's wife, reportedly announced at a party after voicing frustration about her child care.

"Les is an insecure guy with a big ego . . . he had a lot of money but craved respect," the former vice-chair of L Brands, Robert Morosky, would later tell *The Wall Street Journal.*[11] "They played off each other's needs."

The second client, Towers Financial, got Epstein into trouble. Towers would go down as the biggest financial Ponzi scheme in American history prior to Bernie Madoff.

Steven Hoffenberg, who once owned the *New York Post,* ran the company.

"Jeffrey was my partner in what we did raising the billion dollars. He worked with me every day, seven days a week and he was in the mix with everything that I did," said Hoffenberg in an interview with CBS News.[12] "I was the CEO of Towers Financial Corporation, a public company, and Jeffrey was my main assistant, associate, or partner. And the company did do a billion dollars in raising money. And it was criminal."

The way the scheme worked was that Towers Financial would sell bonds and notes, using the proceeds to funnel money to pay interest to earlier accounts. Of course, much of that money went to Hoffenberg himself. Epstein, for his part, was on a retainer pulling in $25,000 a month for his financial advice.

While perpetrating this fraud, Epstein also began a new, relatively low-stakes, but nonetheless revelatory form of fraud, according to those who knew him.[13]

Hoffenberg's Towers Financial tried to take over Pan Am Airways. The point person on the deal ultimately failed Epstein. Upon hearing that an acquaintance of his was traveling to Spain in a few days, Epstein offered, "If you like, I can upgrade you to first class. Much better food."

"How?" asked the acquaintance, the author and journalist Edward Jay Epstein.

"Drop your ticket off with my doorman tomorrow morning. It won't cost you a penny," the financier instructed.

Years later, the writer would recall, "I brought my ticket to the doorman on Friday morning, and Friday evening I picked it up with a first-class sticker and a first-class seat assignment."

Apparently, Jeffrey Epstein had been using stickers procured during the failed Pan Am deal to upgrade friends and acquaintances— without the hassle and expense of actually going through the airlines. It was surprisingly easy to pull off.

The writer recalls that he should have realized then the jig was a fraud, even if it was reflective of his acquaintance. And it couldn't go on forever.

"It was all dazzling fun, but in late 1988 a dark cloud poked its way into the festivities. It began when I tried to board an All Nippon Airways flight that Epstein had upgraded to first class. The A.N.A. representative told me it could not be a first-class ticket, which cost $6,000, because I had paid only $655. When I pointed to the first-class sticker, she said anyone could steal one and paste it in. I was unceremoniously moved to coach," Edward Jay Epstein would write in 2019.

Just as the small-scale fraud came to an end, the large-scale one also did. Hoffenberg ultimately pleaded guilty to $460 million worth of fraud in 1995. "Epstein has remained free and has used and benefited from the ill-gotten gains he amassed as a result of his criminal and fraudulent activities," Hoffenberg, who has been keen in recent years to blame his former associate for the financial crimes, has alleged in court documents.[14]

—

Epstein had now reached the top of his field, finding his way there through a mixture of charm and fraud. He was willing to lie to get what he wanted, and to manipulate powerful people through unknown means into giving him a massive amount of money and power. But was that enough? No, he wanted more.

7
The Accomplice

When Jeffrey Met Ghislaine

If I see somebody he likes, I go over and say, "How would you like to meet a rich man?"

GHISLAINE MAXWELL

I n 1990, Epstein spent $2.5 million on a Palm Beach mansion.[1] The intercoastal waterfront home is an eight-thousand-square-foot, five-bedroom, eight-bathroom stunner, with privacy bushes and a white fence giving cover to the exclusive enclave. The location is prime—less than a mile and a half from Donald Trump's Mar-a-Lago resort, which was purchased five years earlier. It is now estimated to be worth nearly $17 million.

Epstein's rise from Coney Island boy to Upper East Side man had taken less than a decade—with stops at Dalton, Bear Stearns, and then his own shops along the way. He had money and all the luxuries of wealth. Multiple homes, private jets, and beautiful women.

Yet in spite of his newfound wealth, Epstein had a difficult time fitting in with elite society circles. Friends described him as crass with no taste for the arts, food, or culture.

"Palm Beach is a pretty snooty place," said another friend of Epstein's in an interview. "There's no way they were accepting him. Forget all the other things you know about him. He was a lower-middle-class Jew. He was from Coney Island. His father was a Parks Department employee. This guy didn't have an air of class about him. That alone would shun him in Palm Beach."

But Epstein still wanted their acceptance. "Pretension was very important to him," said the friend.

Epstein might have lived among the elites, but he was not one of them. That is, not until he met Ghislaine Maxwell.

Once he met her, his life would change. She introduced him to class, was his match in every way, and would eventually become his partner in one of the darkest schemes one could ever imagine.

—

In the early 1990s, Ghislaine Maxwell was young, popular, and broke. The French-born ninth child of the British media mogul Robert Maxwell, Ghislaine, then in her early thirties, had moved stateside after her father's suspicious passing.

On November 5, 1991, Robert Maxwell, owner of the Mirror Group newspapers in the U.K. and the New York *Daily News,* had been found dead, floating off the Canary Islands, miles from his yacht, *Lady Ghislaine,* named for his reportedly favorite child.[2] Immediately questions arose as to whether he had simply fallen off his boat in the middle of the night, committed suicide, or been killed.

Robert Maxwell had plenty of enemies. His insatiable quest for power and influence led him to raid his companies and banks to help prop up his ever-growing schemes. There were also allegations that he had been a spy—for the Israeli Mossad or for the British or Russian intelligence services. Foreign intelligence services often recruit connected businessmen to become assets or operatives to funnel information on colleagues or political figures they know back to spies. Maxwell, with his transatlantic connections in media, politics, and business, would have been a good recruiting target.

Some thought Maxwell had committed suicide, but his wife maintained that he had not.

In her memoir, *A Mind of My Own*, she revealed that an autopsy discovered "precise details of a whole range of injuries which had been caused before death; there were significant hemorrhages in and around damaged tissues on the back, shoulders, and arms."[3] The report explicitly states, "It is impossible to exclude homicide."

Suicide or not, Ghislaine was left without a father and without resources. The comforts her family fortune afforded her had been wiped out. Especially when it became clear after her father was gone that he had looted hundreds of millions of dollars from the pensions of his company to help cover his debts and keep his empire afloat.

Ghislaine Maxwell had become accustomed to all the trappings of the British elite. With her long, dark wavy hair, she had a way about her that made the men in her life swoon.

But in order to live the life she aspired to, she needed currency. And, given her family's sudden predicament, she needed it quick— and from somewhere else.

—

Despite her father's passing, Ghislaine Maxwell was quick to use his Rolodex and ingratiate herself into America's most elite social circles.

She had helped make inroads into New York City when her father owned the *Daily News*. But now she decided to stay there permanently and make it her home.

"Ghislaine basically didn't have a job, and she went to the opening of anything that had a gold envelope to it," said her friend Laura Goldman in an interview. "She was quite a social person, but part of it was that she wasn't working all day, so she could go to everything."

Ghislaine would party with the movie mogul Harvey Weinstein, the magazine editor Tina Brown, and Arianna Huffington, the socialite wife of a Republican congressman. She was also friends with American royalty (the Clintons) and British royalty (Prince Andrew).[4]

Some called her "Goodtimes Ghislaine," a source told *The Sun*. "She was a huge networker at these bashes, going from famous person to famous person and introducing people who didn't have a prior connection to each other," the source said.[5]

But with her father's passing, she too was missing something—money.

Which is why in the early 1990s Epstein and Ghislaine Maxwell would turn out to be such a durable duo. Each provided what the other one lacked.

"She told me how she had absolutely no money in her pocket and was bawling her eyes out on the streets of New York just prior to meeting Jeffrey," recalled another friend in an interview.

Epstein was very rich and still very much a bachelor. Eva Andersson, the former Miss Sweden and now a doctor, dated Epstein for eleven years before throwing in the towel in the early 1990s. "He really loved her," recalled a friend in an interview. But he had no interest in tying himself down to one woman.

What he was interested in was someone who could help him make his way in posh society. Soon Ghislaine and he would be a couple—and then even more. Maxwell was Epstein's "half ex-girlfriend, half employee, half best friend and fixer," as one acquaintance described it.[6]

According to Epstein's former house manager Juan Alessi, Ghislaine served as both Epstein's girlfriend and the head of his household staff from the mid-1990s until the mid-2000s. "She was the manager of all the households, because he has homes all over the world," he said in a deposition.[7]

The status of their relationship was a mystery even to Epstein's inner circle. "There was a period of time when she was his girlfriend, and then there was a period of time when she was not," said a longtime associate of Epstein's, noting that the precise beginning and end of these periods was unclear.

While the couple often shared a bed and Maxwell acted like his significant other—cooking breakfast for Epstein's overnight guests, accompanying him to social functions—Epstein openly downplayed their romantic involvement. "Nah, she's not my girlfriend; she's just somebody I know," Epstein told one male friend, according to an interview.

Conchita Sarnoff, a journalist and advocate against human trafficking who knew the couple, has said of Maxwell, "She seemed in love when I first saw them together. I believe Jeffrey was taking care of her. I feel Ghislaine clung to Jeffrey because she felt protected by him."[8]

Epstein, Sarnoff said, "seemed less in love but more enamored."

Together their social life flourished. Maxwell introduced Epstein to her friends Prince Andrew and the Duchess of York, her contacts on the New York social scene, and she was on Epstein's arm when he first visited the White House under President Bill Clinton. She also provided Epstein with companionship and real-world lessons on how elites operate.

The relationship was not just based on mutual benefit. Friends said Maxwell was deeply in love with Epstein and hoped to marry him. People close to the couple noted that Epstein shared many characteristics with Maxwell's late father—a serial philanderer with a taste for very young women—whom she had revered from childhood.

Epstein "was her sun and moon," said Maxwell's friend Laura Goldman. "Everything revolved around him."

Privately, Epstein was also deeply protective of his relationship with Maxwell. One longtime friend, who was charmed by the British brunette, recalled asking Epstein if it would be okay to ask her on a date. Epstein said it didn't bother him, and the gentleman took Maxwell out to dinner in New York.

"That was a bad idea," revealed the friend in an interview. "[Jeffrey] didn't talk to me for six months after that."

—

Maxwell fed one of Epstein's needs. It was roughly around this time that he got her to satisfy another. Epstein would provide the money Maxwell desired to live the lifestyle she sought. Maxwell, in turn, would provide young girls for Epstein.

Epstein made no attempt to be monogamous. He always seemed to have a rotation of attractive young women hanging around his homes or accompanying him to parties.

One friend recalled asking Maxwell where Epstein met all these girls in New York. Maxwell took credit for finding them.

"If I see somebody he likes, I go over and say, 'How would you like to meet a rich man?'" claimed Maxwell.

The curious friend asked Maxwell where she slept while Epstein was having sex with these other women.

"I get out of the bedroom," said Maxwell, nonchalantly.

"Maxwell is very clever," the journalist Conchita Sarnoff has observed.[9] "In spite of her personal insecurities, as a result of her father's death and financial challenges, I believe she nevertheless knew exactly what she was doing when she agreed to solicit girls on his behalf. However, I don't think that phase of their relationship began until she understood Epstein would not marry her."

She would accompany him as he jet set across the globe, catering to his every whim. "Every pretty girl in New York, in those days, Ghislaine would invite to Jeffrey's," Maxwell's acquaintance Euan Rellie has said. "Her job was to jazz up his social life by getting fashionable young women to show up."[10]

—

Although it is unclear exactly when Epstein began preying on underage girls, accusers have dated it back over two decades. Numerous victims tell similar tales: they were young, vulnerable, and overpowered by Epstein and his associates.

George Houraney, the director of the American Dream Calendar Girls pageant, said in an interview that he was forced to ban Epstein from his events in the early 1990s after he started preying on the contestants—some of whom were as young as fifteen.

Epstein had started showing up at the pageants in Las Vegas. He was in his late thirties, with a cocky swagger and a business card falsely identifying him as the head of Victoria's Secret.

The contest was a less sophisticated version of Miss America and took place at casinos in Vegas, Atlantic City, and the Bahamas. Hundreds of girls from across the country competed, hoping it would be their ticket to Hollywood stardom or the New York City catwalks.

Unlike Miss America, the contest was open to girls as young as fifteen years old. National winners got cash prizes and were featured in the American Dream Girl bikini calendar, often posting on top of a hot rod.

"The girls that came to me were always young, mostly naive. Some of them had never even been on an airplane," said Houraney in an interview.

"There was no age limit except you had to be fifteen or older, so we had a lot of teens enter," he said. "It was a chance for them to get a scholarship, or money, or whatever, or [try to] get an acting job."

The event had some corporate sponsors, including the men's cologne brand English Leather. Epstein said he wanted to sign on as a backer. But it soon became clear he had another interest in the show.

Houraney said he started getting complaints from girls and their parents. Contestants claimed Epstein promised to help them with their careers and then tried to pressure them into "sexual situations" and badgered them to send him nude photos.

"By the third event, I found out he was trying to get girls in his room and that's against all my rules. Girls weren't allowed in sponsors' rooms or judges' rooms. You know what I mean?" said Houraney. After that, Houraney said he banned Epstein from the events.

But this didn't dissuade Epstein. Houraney said he ran into him later at an American Dream Calendar Girls party hosted by Donald

Trump at Mar-a-Lago. Trump had partnered with the beauty pageant through his Trump Taj Mahal casino in Atlantic City.

According to Houraney, the party was supposed to be a meet and greet for American Dream girls and representatives of beauty brands, such as Revlon and Max Factor. He said Trump's staff handled the guest list, and Epstein was the only "sponsor" who was actually invited.

"In walked Jeffrey Epstein, and I had a fit," said Houraney. "He thought because he's now friends with Trump, and I'm producing events at Trump's [casino], that he can just buy Trump and still get into my events."

Furious, Houraney said he pulled Epstein aside.

"You know, you can't keep doing this. You're going to get arrested," Houraney told him.

Epstein laughed it off.

"I've got enough money to get out of anything I ever need," Epstein responded, according to Houraney. "There's plenty of countries I can live in like a king and I don't have to worry."

All the same, perhaps it was after this that Epstein decided that his and Maxwell's ordinary efforts to procure young women were not enough and began what would become their notorious pyramid scheme for preying on underage girls.

—

It worked like this: Epstein or someone working on his behalf would solicit a young girl to come to his house or where he was staying to give him a "massage." The unsuspecting victim-in-waiting would nearly always be from a poor or otherwise disadvantaged background.

She'd be offered a chance to make, say, $200 giving a "massage," wherein she'd be sexually coerced or assaulted by Epstein. Depending on how much sexual gratification she gave him, she'd be paid more.

But on some occasions the girl would not succumb to Epstein's demands. That would be okay, too, so long as she in turn recruited other girls from her peer group who in her place would perform on demand. In fact, every girl had the opportunity to make more money this way. With the payment for recruiting being the same as for being sexually violated, both became options. They could themselves service Epstein or recruit other kids to the cause. The ideal scenario, in Epstein's eyes, was for a girl to do both.

Which all helps explain why Epstein targeted girls from low-income families. They were more attracted to the idea of getting paid $200. Perhaps not an exorbitant sum, but an amount of money they had no other opportunity to obtain for an hour's work. Additionally, their friends—and their friends' friends—could also more easily fall prey to the financier. There was another bonus, perhaps, that Epstein and his consorts had in mind when they plotted their devilish scam. Lower-class kids would be less likely to be believed by law enforcement and adults.

Epstein's appetite was so ferocious he would, at his height, require "massages" three times a day. Moreover, he craved variety and youth.

"He told me he wanted them as young as I could find them," a victim who claimed to have recruited at least seventy girls would tell the *Miami Herald*.[11] "He wanted as many girls as I could get him. It was never enough."

Meeting Epstein's needs required a significant operation. His house staffers, including Maxwell, his assistant Sarah Kellen, and his butler Alfredo Rodriguez, were needed to help keep the system running.

"He explained to me that, in his opinion, he needed to have three orgasms a day. It was biological, like eating," said Johanna Sjoberg, a woman who was in her early twenties when she started giving Epstein sexual massages.[12]

The phone memos found by police in the house make it clear that his employees spent a large portion of their days trying to help feed his sexual appetites.

Many of the notes, written by household staffers, document phone messages from young girls and attempts to schedule Epstein's "sessions." "She is wondering if 2:30 is okay cus she needs to stay in school," read one phone memo in February 2005.

Prior to 2003, the recruiting of girls was handled primarily by Ghislaine Maxwell, according to Epstein's house manager Juan Alessi and others. Maxwell often passed out business cards to pretty girls at spas and on college campuses.

"Ms. Maxwell was the one that recruited," said Alessi in a court deposition. "I remember one occasion or two occasions she would say to me, [Juan], give me a list of all the spas in Palm Beach County, and I will drive her from one to the other to PGA in Boca; and she would go in and drop 20 . . . business cards," he said. "Was never, never done by me or Mr. Epstein or anyone else that I know of."

Alessi said Maxwell was demanding and would often make him drive her up and down the coast to search for girls to hire.

"She was rotten spoiled and she tried to drive the house like a palace and not a home," he said.

Although Maxwell was Epstein's girlfriend at the time, she seemed eager to bring in additional women for him, according to Sjoberg.

"She let me know that she was—she would not be able to please [Epstein] as much as he needed and that is why there were other girls around," said Sjoberg in a court deposition.

—

As Epstein was finding his way in a new social class, he had found a partner to help navigate this new world. Together, with Maxwell, he was able to satisfy his social needs and sexual desires.

But Maxwell's friend Goldman said the British socialite never gave up hope that her relationship with Epstein would one day have a degree of normalcy.

"I guess she kept thinking if she brought one more girl, did one more thing, that he would marry her," said Goldman in an interview. "She really thought that he would marry her in the end. She always, always, always believed that."

8

The Victims

Preying on the Vulnerable

No, he really had some kind of contempt for women.

A GOOD FRIEND OF JEFFREY EPSTEIN'S

I've got enough money to get out of anything I ever need.

JEFFREY EPSTEIN

R oyal Palm Beach High School in West Palm Beach is twelve miles from Epstein's waterfront mansion, but it might as well be a world away. The thin strip of land between the Intracoastal Waterway and the shimmering white beaches a short walk to the east is the waterfront home to the elites—the Epsteins, the Trumps, the Bill Gateses, the Tiger Woodses of the world. Cross the giant bridges under which yachts pass, and you start going inland, where the farther west you get, the more the surrounding areas are populated by the people who serve the wealthy who live on the beaches and canals.

It was inland where the kids of housemaids, groundskeepers, and law enforcement lived. It was "ground zero," as *The Palm Beach Post* would put it, for Epstein's sick pyramid scheme.[1]

"These girls had never even been to Palm Beach island," the victim attorney Adam Horowitz told the newspaper. "Some of them were living in trailer parks. This was a whole new world to them."

Epstein, who himself had to cross the Brooklyn Bridge to begin to rise up in the world, was no stranger to how people from a lower financial class might react to a made man with a wad of cash. He would use this power differential to maximize his own pleasure. Those stories are shocking.

—

One Sunday in the winter of 2005, a fourteen-year-old girl named Amanda (not her real name) told her dad she was going shopping with her friend Haley Robson in West Palm Beach. Haley picked up Amanda at her dad's house in a red pickup truck. The girls didn't tell Amanda's father what they were planning to do first—stop by the house of Haley's boss, an "old man" in Palm Beach, to pick up some money.

"The old man's gonna give us both money so we can go shopping," Haley reportedly told Amanda.

Amanda had a vague idea that they would have to do *something* for the money. "I knew something was wrong, nobody's just gonna pay you money," she told police later. But her friend Haley, who was several years older, had told her only that they would be getting $200 each. To Amanda, who made $6 an hour at her part-time job at Chick-fil-A, this was a fortune.

In a subsequent police interview, Amanda described the events that followed.

The girls listened to music on the drive, singing along to the radio. They crossed over the bridge to Palm Beach, past Worth Avenue, the town's posh bougainvillea- and palm-lined main street with storefronts advertising Chanel and Louis Vuitton. They followed A1A past the Everglades Club, through neighborhoods shielded by towering boxwoods, and finally turned onto the narrow cul-de-sac of El Brillo Way.

Haley's boss, Jeffrey Epstein, lived in the house at the end of the road, an unadorned, boxy white mansion with a security gate. The gate opened when the girls drove up, and they were ushered into the house by one of Epstein's female assistants.

Haley made herself at home in the kitchen, chatting with Epstein and his house staff. Meanwhile, Epstein's female assistant motioned for Amanda to follow her upstairs.

"I thought Haley . . . was gonna get paid in like, you know, private," Amanda told police later. "So I went upstairs."

Epstein's assistant took her up to the master bathroom, where there was a massage table. She told Amanda that the fourteen-year-old would be giving Epstein a massage, placed several bottles of lotion on a nearby table, and then left the room.

After about five minutes, Epstein entered.

"Hi, I'm Jeff," said the man. Amanda noticed that he had graying hair and a long horsey face. "I'll be right back," he told her. "You can take off your clothes."

Amanda was uncomfortable. She wondered why Haley had stayed downstairs. She took off her shirt but kept her bra and pants on. When Epstein came back into the room, wearing a towel, he was noticeably annoyed.

"No, I meant get naked," he said sternly. "Take off your pants." There was an edge to his voice. The fourteen-year-old took off her pants, but kept her underwear and bra on.

Epstein dropped his towel and lay down naked on the massage table. The girl rubbed lotion on his shoulders in circles, trying not to look at his hairy back.

"Where do you go to school?" he asked her.

"Wellington High School," she told him.

"How do you know Haley?" he asked.

"She's my boyfriend's cousin," said Amanda, who had been dating her first boyfriend, Chris (not his real name), a baseball player at her school, for three weeks. "How do *you* know Haley?"

"She's been working for me for a long time," said Epstein. He paused. "It would feel more comfortable if you got on my back," he said.

Amanda looked at his back. There was a thick line of hair running down it to his buttocks. "Gross," she thought. She climbed tentatively onto the massage table, putting one knee on either side of him and kneeling to avoid touching his bare skin with her underwear.

"Sit on me," he insisted. "Put all your weight on me."

Mortified, the fourteen-year-old girl did as he told her. She continued to massage his back in circles, and Epstein started to moan. He turned over onto his back and ordered her to rub his chest while he groped her hips. She tried not to look down, but she could see he was masturbating.

"I didn't know what else to do," she told police later. "I just felt intimidated."

After what seemed like an eternity, he wiped himself off with a towel. He paid her $300 in cash and told her to leave her phone number with his assistant.

"You can see yourself out," he said.

Amanda left the room. Later she would recount wandering through the maze of hallways for a while, unable to remember how to get back downstairs.

—

Haley Robson, Amanda's friend, recruited multiple underage victims for Epstein for the $200 commission. Robson had started working for Epstein as a teenager and told police that she preferred bringing new girls to him rather than performing sex acts herself. She said Epstein made it clear that he was interested only in girls in their teens and very early twenties. Once, when she brought a twenty-three-year-old, Epstein told her the woman was "too old."

Haley wasn't the only victim who also recruited. "I brought girls I didn't like and really, frankly, did not give a shit about," said one of Epstein's sixteen-year-old victims in a police interview. "Girls that I knew were skanks that would do anything. Who, like, girls that would just like suck dick in the bathroom at school. Like not even people that I was friends with, I'd just hear a rumor about a girl and be like hey I know a way you can make two hundred dollars."

Epstein's house manager, Juan Alessi, recalled seeing more than a hundred women visit Epstein to give him massages in the years he worked there.

"We have a table—massage table in basically every room, guest room," said Alessi. He said Epstein received up to three massages a day, and estimated that the house went through forty or fifty towels each day and had "gallons" of massage oils and lubricants.

He said he saw sex toys in Epstein's sink after some of the massages. "It was a long dick, I think. Rubber thing," he said.

There were always young women around the house. One, a shy Yugoslavian blond girl named Nadia, was his live-in "number one girlfriend" in the middle of the first decade of the twenty-first century, according to a police interview with Epstein's former house manager Alfredo Rodriguez. Epstein claimed that she was his sex slave and he had purchased her from her parents.

"[Nadia] told me that she came from Yugoslavia when she was, like, fifteen, with Jeffrey," recalled one victim named Jennifer (not her real name) in a police interview.

Jennifer was sixteen years old and working at the Hollister store in West Palm Beach, trying to save money for a camping trip to Maine, when one of her co-workers asked her if she wanted to make some quick cash.

"You can get a plane ticket in two hours," the girl told Jennifer, according to a police interview. "We can go and give this guy a massage, and, um, he'll pay two hundred dollars for like forty-five minutes or an hour."

The sixteen-year-old started going to Epstein's house regularly to give him "massages" that quickly morphed into explicit sexual encounters. She told police in an interview, during which she broke down crying at multiple points, that she was with him "hundreds" of times over a two-year period.

"The way it went was if you worked there for the first like three times, you got paid $200," said Jennifer. "After that, if you were persistent and worked all the time, it was on average $300. Sometimes I got paid $1,000."

The money "was a lot for a sixteen-year-old girl making six bucks an hour," she said.

Jennifer said Epstein would offer her additional money for letting him use sex toys on her. He also paid her to have sex with his girlfriend Nadia.

"Sometimes he got violent," she recalled. "He pulled my hair a lot harder than it should have been pulled . . . he would pull it to where it would rip my hair out. It would rip my hair, and then sometimes he would pick me up and like throw me whichever way he wanted me, and then he would just like use a toy or like his hand or whatever."

After some encounters she said it was painful for her to walk because of how aggressive Epstein was with sex toys.

"He would get really rough and I'd get cut . . . like ripped a little bit," she said.

Jennifer said she never had sexual intercourse with Epstein and suggested that he might have been unable to perform sexually.

"[His penis was] really fat at the bottom and skinny at the top where it's attached. And, he can never get fully hard, ever," she said. "I don't know if that's some sort of thing that's wrong with him, but it definitely was not normal."

She said she stopped seeing Epstein after two years because her boyfriend asked her to stop. But she said she did not want to completely sever ties.

"If I called him today he would give me as much money as I asked him for," she told police. "He doesn't know that I hate him the way I do."

━━

The number of girls Epstein victimized could be as high as the hundreds, and there are many who have declined to speak about it publicly. But the most outspoken and now well known is Virginia Roberts Giuffre, who was one of the first to go public with details about her alleged experiences with Epstein and his associates.

Giuffre was around seventeen years old working at Mar-a-Lago in Palm Beach when she met Ghislaine Maxwell. Giuffre was a spa attendant at the exclusive club owned by Donald Trump. Her dad, a well-respected maintenance worker at the resort, had connected her with the job.

"While reading a book about anatomy, Ghislaine Maxwell, met me at the spa, not having an education or anything behind me, I thought this was a great opportunity to work for her . . . to make some extra money and learn about massage. So, I went to Jeffrey's mansion about five or six that afternoon," Giuffre has said in a proffer.[2]

Her own dad drove her to the Palm Beach mansion, just a mile and a half away. "[Maxwell] led me upstairs into Jeffrey's bedroom past Jeffrey's massage room that has a steam room, shower and massage table," she said. "There is actually an extra room that has—that nobody knows about—a kind of secret room and it's got a whole bunch of pictures of pornographic literature and sex toys."

Epstein "was lying naked on top of the massage table." He dictated what she should do. First "it was actually a real massage."

Then, Giuffre alleges, "Ghislaine who had stayed in the room told me to undress and began to take off my shirt and skirt—that is—my white Mar-a-Lago uniform." Maxwell then undressed herself.

At this point, the girl was scared. "I was expected to lick his nipples and give him oral sex while he fondled me and then at the end I was told by Ghislaine to get on top and straddle Jeffrey sexually."

Laura Goldman, Ghislaine's friend, said she believed Ghislaine's involvement was less about sex and more about asserting her position as Epstein's "main" girlfriend.

"I really, really believe that she was there to tell [the girls], 'He's my man.' She wasn't there for the girls," said Goldman. "She was trying to mark her territory, or domination, or whatever."

Epstein immediately took a liking to Giuffre. "So you're a bad girl in a good girl's body," he told her, according to Giuffre's 2011 account in the *Daily Mail*. She said Epstein gifted her an "absolutely beautiful" Palm Beach pad. But of course there was a catch; she had to be on call. All the time.

She even began traveling with Epstein, according to flight records. She'd stay with him on his trips and very occasionally in a spare room at his Palm Beach mansion.

So insecure was Epstein about himself that he used to brag to his victims about preying on other children, said Giuffre. "The worst story I heard directly from his own mouth was about these pretty 12-year-old girls he had flown in, transported to Palm Beach by somebody else, for his birthday," Giuffre said.

"I did see them. I did meet them. Jeffrey bragged after he met them they were 12 years old and flown over from France because they are really poor over there, and their parents needed the money or whatever. That was the worst. He was constantly bragging about the girls' ages or where he got them from or about their past and how terrible their past was and good he is making it for them," according to Giuffre.

Giuffre has said the quality of the massages, though they always ended sexually, was actually important to Epstein. And in fact, he wanted her to become a better masseuse, so he sent her to Thailand to improve her skills so that she could then return better able to serve her master.

But Giuffre used the trip to Thailand for something else. Days into her trip she met her future husband and decided she would never return to Epstein's servitude. Within a week, they would marry.

9
The Perps

pstein's sexual abuse of Giuffre also extended to him "lending" her out to his elite circle of friends, she publicly alleged in media interviews and court documents years after she cut ties with him. In a 2015 Florida district court filing as part of a civil lawsuit against the U.S. government, Giuffre claimed Epstein "sexually trafficked" her to "politically-connected and financially-powerful people" in order to "ingratiate himself with them for business, personal, political, and financial gain, as well as to obtain potential blackmail information." Giuffre said Ghislaine Maxwell was the "primary co-conspirator in his sexual abuse and sex trafficking scheme." Epstein allegedly began trafficking Giuffre to his friends about two years after they met, she told the *Mail on Sunday* in her first press interview in 2011.[1]

"I would give the massage, I would go home, and the next day when I saw Jeffrey, he would pay me for what I did," Giuffre has said.[2] She said Epstein's only instruction for her was to "treat them like you treat me."

"I complied with what he wanted because . . . it was just very mind-boggling how I let him have so much control or power over me," she has recalled.

Giuffre claimed Epstein used the opportunity to get dirt on various high-profile people. "I always reported back to Jeffrey about what happened after I provided massages to his friends," said Giuffre.

"Jeffrey would have a laugh with me a few times about some of their different mannerisms, I guess you would say, like some of them, one guy had a foot fetish and that was really weird and I mentioned it to Jeffrey and we had a laugh over it."

She claimed Epstein relished the fact that he had dirt on his friends. "Lots of people owed him favors from what he told me. He's got everybody in his pocket, and he would laugh about how he helps people for the sole purpose—in the end—to owe him something. That's why I believe he does so many favors in the first place."

According to Giuffre, this included the former president of the United States, who had a relationship with Epstein. To be clear: Giuffre herself has never made any accusation that she engaged in sexual activities, or even a non-sensual massage, with Bill Clinton. Yet she distinctly remembers asking Epstein why Clinton was hanging around.

"Well, he owes me a favor," Giuffre says Epstein told her.[3] She went on to add, "They're all in each other's pockets."

—

Epstein did little to hide his interest in young women from friends, neighbors, and household staff. If anything, he flaunted it.

"At his house [in Palm Beach], there were always more girls than you could count," said one friend in an interview. "I always counted like three or four. What they were doing there I couldn't tell . . . They weren't walking around naked, they weren't making sexual overtures, they were talking . . . They sounded and looked like college girls."

He enjoyed bike riding, and sometimes he'd be spotted cycling around Palm Beach with half a dozen young women trailing after him. The sight no doubt shocked the tiny island's old-money residents.

But many people wanted in on his victims. And Epstein had done what he could to be able to play gracious host. By 1998, he had become so monstrously wealthy that his New York City townhome and Palm Beach mansion were not enough. So he bought an island.

Operating as the sole proprietor of L.S.J. LLC, Epstein purchased Little St. James for $7.95 million. In due time, it would be widely referred to as Little St. Jeff and then later as Orgy Island or Sex Island or Pedophile Island.

The seventy-two-acre island is a lovely tropical getaway and, most attractively to its new owner, completely private. "You can hop off a plane and never see anybody again," the venture capitalist Arch Cummin, the former owner, said upon the sale.[4]

Onshore, there was a main house, three smaller guesthouses, a separate cottage for staff, and a helipad. Getting there was made easier by Epstein's use of his private plane, which he'd fly into St. Thomas and then take his helicopter over.

The investment apparently paid off. Not only did the island rise significantly in value (it is now estimated to be worth north of $60 million), but he also picked up a ranch in New Mexico and an apartment in Paris.

The island and his new properties allowed him to entertain more freely, sharing his victims with those who might be able to do him a favor.

—

Phone messages eventually recovered by the police hint at some of the people who at the very least knew of Epstein's activities. One particularly disturbing memo from September 2005 was a phone message from Epstein's close friend Jean-Luc Brunel, a French modeling agent.

"[Jean Luc] has a teacher for you to teach you how to speak Russian. She is 2x8 years old. Not blonde. Lessons are free and you can have 1st today if you call," said the note.[5]

Brunel ran a modeling business with cash provided by Epstein. Giuffre has accused Brunel of providing underage girls to Epstein as part of his sick sexual pyramid scheme and human trafficking operation.

"Brunel would offer the girls 'modeling' jobs. A lot of the girls came from poor countries or poor backgrounds, and he lured them in with a promise of making good money," Giuffre has said in legal documents.[6]

Phone messages, which were scribbled down in a memo pad by Epstein's staff, were later collected through trash pulls by police investigators. The memos provide a glimpse into Epstein's wide circle of influential contacts.

The media tycoon Mort Zuckerman, the longtime owner of the New York *Daily News*, called to ask for "the address of the house to 'drop by' tomorrow at 10:45 a.m.," said one note on January 22, 2005.

There were also messages from the embattled media mogul Harvey Weinstein—"Returning your call"; Senator George Mitchell—"Return a call"; and Donald Trump.

Trump had a friendship with Epstein in the early days, but it eventually fell apart. In the early 2000s, Trump banned Epstein from his exclusive Mar-a-Lago club in Palm Beach after hearing that he had propositioned a member's underage daughter.

"It wasn't only Virginia [Giuffre], which would have been bad enough for Trump. It was a complaint from a member's daughter," said Sam Nunberg, Trump's 2016 political adviser, in an interview.

Nunberg said he asked Trump for details about his prior relationship with Epstein in 2015, warning him that it could become a campaign liability.

"Trump told me [Epstein] was a 'member,' he was a 'client.' Meaning that the extent that Trump was familiar or hung out with him was because [Epstein] gave him money," said Nunberg. "He said, 'I kicked him out when this stuff became public, and he's completely banned from my properties. He's a real sicko.'"

Not all of the men who left messages seemed to recognize that raping underage girls was the work of a "sicko."

David Copperfield, the celebrity magician, left at least ten phone messages with Epstein in January 2005. "I just want to say hello," read one note. Another simply said, "It's jackpot." The two also appeared to discuss Epstein's scheduled attendance at one of Copperfield's shows later that month.

One of Epstein's alleged victims claimed he persuaded her to fly to Las Vegas with him to see a performance by a "world-famous" magician when she was just fifteen years old in 2004. She said Epstein took her backstage to meet the performer. Epstein later sexually assaulted her, she claimed.

"Epstein and/or his agents had arranged for the girls to go backstage and meet the performer, along with several other young girls whom Epstein had arranged to be there," said a lawsuit filed by the alleged victim against Epstein's estate last November. "For a girl from the Midwest, all of this was like a dream come true—to be flown around in private jets, to meet a world-famous performer backstage, and to be among other beautiful girls, almost all of whom were much older than her. She felt like she was being treated special, and like a grown up."

Gloria Allred, an attorney for the alleged victim, said she was unable to comment on whether the magician referenced in the lawsuit was Copperfield.

Epstein would also be pegged as close to other important politicians and academics—Senator George Mitchell, Governor Bill Richardson, Nobel Prize winners, and Harvard and Princeton professors.

Virginia Roberts Giuffre, the same victim who has accused Epstein and Prince Andrew of sexual wrongdoing, has claimed that the former Senate majority leader, a Democrat from Maine, sexually abused her. She described some of the alleged encounters she had with Epstein's associates in her unpublished book manuscript that was included in court records as part of a 2015 defamation lawsuit she filed against Ghislaine Maxwell. In a subsequent court filing, Giuffre's attorneys described the manuscript as a "fictionalized account of what happened to her" written as "an act of empowerment and a way of reframing and taking control over the narrative of her past abuse that haunts her."[7]

"My body was put on the banquet menu . . . for a powerful senator, George Mitchell, and another prominent Nobel Prize winning scientist," Giuffre wrote in the unpublished book manuscript, where she retells how Epstein kept her as his sex slave for his pleasure and for his friends. "They would be only some of the recognizable figures of the high society that became added to my list of clientele."

Giuffre's claim against Mitchell, unlike the ones against Epstein,

Ghislaine Maxwell, and Prince Andrew, was made less compelling by the fact that she does not provide the very details that make her other accusations so believable.

Ironically, and perhaps disastrously, Mitchell had been serving on the board of the compensation fund of the Archdiocese of Philadelphia for victims of sexual abuse by priests,[8] a posting that has been scrutinized since these allegations emerged.

Mitchell has denied these claims. "I have never met, spoken with, or had any contact with Ms. Giuffre," Mitchell told the press in a statement. "In my contacts with Mr. Epstein, I never observed or suspected any inappropriate conduct with underage girls. I only learned about his actions when they were reported in the media related to his prosecution in Florida. We have had no further contact."[9]

Similar claims by Giuffre were made against the former New Mexico governor Bill Richardson, the modeling agent Jean-Luc Brunel, the lawyer Alan Dershowitz, and the financier Glenn Dubin, whose wife, Eva Andersson-Dubin, used to date Epstein.[10]

Most of the accused have denied Giuffre's allegations. And only Dershowitz, who has never been known to be silent or reserved about anything, has gone so far as to launch a public rebuttal campaign with the aim of clearing his name once and for all.

Dershowitz, the Democratic lawyer who more recently defended President Donald Trump in his impeachment trial on the floor of the Senate in the beginning of 2020, went so far as to publish a book on just this subject, *Guilt by Accusation: The Challenge of Proving Innocence in the Age of #MeToo*.[11]

"It feels terrible. Fifty-five years of public service," he said in an interview. "I'm eighty-one years old. I'll probably spend the rest of my life in and out of court."

Giuffre said she was forced to have sexual relations with the prominent attorney on multiple occasions, including in a stretch limousine and on Epstein's private island.

"One such powerful individual that Epstein forced then-minor [Giuffre] to have sexual relations with was former Harvard Law Professor Alan Dershowitz, a close friend of Epstein's and well-known criminal defense attorney," said a December 2014 court filing by Giuffre's attorneys as part of a victims' rights lawsuit against the government. "Epstein required [Giuffre] to have sexual relations with Dershowitz on numerous occasions while she was a minor, not only in Florida but also on private planes, in New York, New Mexico, and the U.S. Virgin Islands. In addition to being a participant in the abuse of Jane Doe #3 and other minors, Dershowitz was an eye-witness to the sexual abuse of many other minors by Epstein and several of Epstein's co-conspirators."

Dershowitz has vehemently denied Giuffre's allegations and says he never met her. He has released travel and credit card records disputing that he was in the places she claimed he was when the alleged encounters occurred. He has also highlighted discrepancies in Giuffre's accounts that he believes undermine her credibility; for example, she previously said she was fifteen when she met Epstein, while employment records indicate she likely met Epstein when she was sixteen or seventeen.

He noted that she also did not claim she had relations with him in a 2011 memoir manuscript that she pitched to publishers, which included accounts of alleged sexual encounters she had with other associates of Epstein's. In the draft, Giuffre also said she went to a dinner party with Bill Clinton on Epstein's island, a story that appears to conflict with Secret Service records. Giuffre's attorneys have said the manuscript was a "fictionalized account" of her experiences.

The situation has spawned a complicated web of litigation. Giuffre is currently suing Dershowitz for defamation. Dershowitz, meanwhile, has taken legal action against both her and her attorney David Boies. He claims Boies persuaded Giuffre to accuse him as part of a wider plot to shake down Epstein's benefactor, the billionaire Leslie Wexner, for money.

But Giuffre's claims would spark years of media attention and provide on-the-record testimony alleging sexual trafficking of girls. It was a charge that would stick in the court of public opinion, even if legal proceedings would prove to be far more forgiving.

10
How He Got Away the First Time

After he had operated for about a decade with impunity, trouble began to brew for Jeffrey Epstein. In 2005, the Palm Beach County Police Department opened an investigation into Epstein after receiving a phone call from a concerned stepmother. The concerned parent called the cops, on March 14 of that year, claiming her stepchild, a fourteen-year-old Royal Palm Beach High student, had been the victim of molestation.

By October 20, 2005, the investigation had developed to the point where investigators had probable cause. They executed a search warrant at his residence but were surprised to see that electronic equipment, like computers, was no longer on the premises. Was the suspected perpetrator given a heads-up?

Many inside the police department believe it's a distinct possibility. Epstein had worked hard to win the allegiance of local law enforcement, perhaps even enough to get them to look away most of the time. He had, after all, given $50,000 to the Palm Beach Police Scholarship Fund around 2001. Then, in 2003, he gave an additional $36,000 to the Town of Palm Beach. And an additional donation on December 14,

2004, of $90,000 to the Palm Beach Police Department for the purchase of equipment.[1]

As Palm Beach police finalized their case and prepared to obtain a search warrant for Epstein's house in October 2005, Epstein received a late night phone call from a longtime aide to one of his close associates, Bill Clinton.

Sandy Berger—Clinton's former national security adviser—left an urgent message for Epstein to call him back. "Can you call [Berger] at this number between 10 and 10:30 p.m.?" read the memo on October 2, 2005.

There is no indication of what Berger, who passed away in 2015, wanted to discuss that night. The next morning, when police pulled trash from Epstein's house—as they had surreptitiously been doing for months—they found a broken sex toy in the garbage, according to the detectives' notes.

"Inside of one of the [white garbage bags], I located a broken piece of a hard plastic or clear acrylic stick, which was shaped with small ridges," said the notes from the Palm Beach police detectives that day.[2] "This device is commonly used as a sexual toy which is inserted into the vagina or anus for stimulation."

The timing of the call stood out to the victims' attorneys. In a deposition of Epstein's assistant Adriana Ross, one of the victims' lawyers, Brad Edwards, asked whether Berger tipped Epstein off to the looming search warrant.

"[Berger] called the house within three weeks of the search warrant being executed. Did he tip off Jeffrey Epstein?" asked Edwards.[3] Ross, who was exercising her Fifth Amendment right against self-incrimination, refused to answer.

By April 2006, Epstein had hired goons to help him deal with his problem, and potential witnesses were beginning to feel the heat. The message was clear, one victim's father would report, relaying the message he heard to prosecutors: "Those who help him will be compensated, and those who hurt him will be dealt with."[4]

Epstein's attorneys besieged prosecutors with documents, including reports on potential drug use by his underage accusers and the alleged criminal backgrounds of their parents.

Epstein's legal team even obtained confidential internal reports from one of the girls' employers, Victoria's Secret—the company owned by Epstein's longtime benefactor, Leslie Wexner—that claimed the teenager had been fired for theft.

In one letter to the assistant state attorney's office, Epstein's lawyers made their intentions clear. His team was fully prepared to shred his accuser's reputation in front of the grand jury.

"Thank you for giving Mr. Epstein the opportunity to present information to the Grand Jury. Enclosed please find background information on [redacted victim's name] and her family," the letter read. "You will find the enclosed information presents [redacted victim] as someone who is untruthful, sexually active, smokes marijuana, drinks alcohol, and shoplifts regularly.

"Additionally, the information reveals the motive behind the false allegations," the letter continued. "Based on Ms. [redacted's] lack of credibility, we request that you reconsider your decision to present this matter to the Grand Jury. In support of this request, it is important to acknowledge that Mr. Epstein does not use drugs or alcohol and has an unequivocal reputation for being truthful; a strict contrast to Ms. [redacted's] reputation. I look forward to hearing from you after you have had a chance to review this information."

Epstein that month reached a deal with the state attorney of Palm

Beach County to plead guilty, which resulted in the cancellation of the scheduled grand jury. The deal appeared too lenient to the Palm Beach police chief, Michael Reiter, especially after he caught wind of the fact that Epstein had hired as his counsel the husband of the top prosecutor in the state attorney's office. It stank.

In July 2006, a local grand jury convened and heard the testimony of only a single victim—a fourteen-year-old girl who accused the rich resident of molestation. Epstein was subsequently placed under arrest but soon freed after posting the measly $3,000 bond.

Reiter was furious. He realized Epstein was circumventing the law and likely to get off with nothing more than a slap on the wrist. In a rare move, he sent a letter to the victim's parents letting them know that he was referring the case to the FBI.

"I do not believe justice has been sufficiently served by the indictment that has been issued," said Reiter in the letter. "Therefore, please know that this matter has been referred to the Federal Bureau of Investigation to determine if violations of federal law have occurred."

Within weeks, the feds took over the case. In almost no time they found three dozen more alleged victims. The federal prosecutor in charge of the office handling the case was Alexander Acosta, an attorney formerly in the private practice Kirkland & Ellis.

Epstein meanwhile altered his tactics, hiring lawyers from Acosta's former law firm to represent him as he dealt with the feds. They would know Acosta, and maybe, just maybe, they could get him out of the fix that the FBI had landed him in. "These were very high-profile lawyers. And they put a lot of pressure to bear on [Acosta] to work out some kind of a plea agreement, even though at the same time the plea negotiations were going on, the FBI was uncovering more and more evidence that Epstein's crimes went far beyond Palm Beach, that he possibly was operating an international sex trafficking organization, in which he had recruiters overseas," the reporter Julie K. Brown, a *Miami Herald* investigative reporter, said in an interview with Democracy Now![5]

"And so, there were two parallel things going on: the FBI working the case at the same time that Alex Acosta and his team were trying to make the case go away, so to speak, by negotiating some kind of a plea bargain."

When a deal was finally struck between Epstein's lawyers and Acosta, over a friendly breakfast at a Miami hotel, the financier was effectively able to shut down the growing investigation. That was the effect of the non-prosecution agreement, signed September 24, 2007. In exchange, Epstein would avoid federal charges and agree to prostitution charges with the Palm Beach County state attorney.

The deal was a major victory for Epstein. But he didn't see it that way, according to his attorney at the time, Alan Dershowitz.

"If the full extent of his activities were known when he made that deal, I don't think he would have gotten that deal," said Dershowitz.

"He didn't think I got a good deal for him . . . For a while he complained about the bills and had them audited by his accountant and stuff like that. Ultimately, we compromised and he never paid me the full amount he owed me."

It was true that the prostitution charges would carry a negative stigma for Epstein, but a far less severe one than child rape and sex trafficking, which is what he almost certainly would have faced had the Federal Bureau of Investigation been given the leeway to carry on their own investigation to its conclusion. Besides, the FBI investigation had been rapidly expanding. Agents not only had been investigating his Florida home but also had been traveling to New York and New

Mexico to get a better handle on the lascivious and illegal activity he had been engaging in at his numerous residences across America.

So on June 30, 2008, more than three years after the initial complaint from the worried stepmother was lodged with the local police department, Jeffrey Epstein pleaded guilty to two charges: soliciting a prostitute and soliciting prostitution of a minor. He was sentenced to eighteen months at the Palm Beach County jail's private wing, where minor and low-risk inmates were housed.

But Epstein proved even more crafty, using his influence and money effectively to buy an even more cushy sentence.

"I visited him once in prison . . . because he needed advice about what level he had to register in New York [as a sex offender]," said Dershowitz in an interview. "He was very encouraged, optimistic. He's a likable guy and everybody in the prison liked him. They got along; everybody was just nice to him. He didn't do hard time. But nobody does, if you get that kind of a sentence."

Another friend who visited him said in an interview that Epstein "actually lived in his own part of the jail nobody else was in. It was like a luxury jail."

The work-release program Epstein managed to finagle made the sentence an inconvenience rather than a severe punishment. It allowed the now admitted sexual predator to go to work for at times fourteen hours a day. So in the morning he would get picked up by a waiting chauffeur who'd drive him to a Palm Beach office building. Fourteen hours later, after a full day away at the office, he would be driven back to jail, where he would spend the night. And believe it or not, he was working overtime—six days a week.

While in jail, Epstein boasted to a friend that he was in negotiations to buy a portion of the Miami Dolphins from the then owner,

Wayne Huizenga, according to an interview. Epstein, who knew and cared nothing about sports, mused, "I think if you buy them, you worry about hot dog sales."

The friend also recalled one jail visit that Epstein cut short by telling him, "It's 4:00 p.m., I'm expecting a call from Israel, from the prime minister." At that hour, it would have been nearing midnight in Tel Aviv.

So sweet was Epstein's deal that he was able to receive his "massages" even while serving time. They were carried out at his office, instead of his mansion, though it is believed that they came with all the benefits of the ones that got him into the joint in the first place.

"It was not for some business arrangement and it was for . . . improper sexual contact," Brad Edwards, a lawyer representing accusers, told the *Daily Beast*.

"He just wasn't in jail. He only slept there. He was in his office most of the day and what I can tell you he had visitors, female visitors," the lawyer told the website.

"They believed they were going there for something other than a sexual purpose. Once there, he used his perfect master manipulation to turn the situation into something sexual," said the lawyer.[6]

And this is why, when Epstein finally did die in jail, so many were inclined to believe he was murdered. After all, he had a history of beating the courts. And he had powerful presidents and princes in his pocket who could help him out in a time of need.

11
The Prince

Transatlantic Travels with Andrew

*Jeffrey's my friend. Being loyal to your friends is a virtue. And
I'm going to be loyal to him.*

PRINCE ANDREW

The New York literary agent John Brockman described a scene he
once walked in on when he went to Epstein's Upper East Side
mansion.

"Last time I visited his house (the largest private residence in NYC),
I walked in to find him in a sweatsuit and a British guy in a suit with
suspenders, getting foot massages from two young well-dressed Russian women [one apparently named Irina]. After grilling me for a
while about cyber-security, the Brit, named Andy, was commenting
on the Swedish authorities and the charges against Julian Assange,"
Brockman wrote in an email to a client for whom he was trying to facilitate a meeting with his financial patron, Jeffrey Epstein.

According to Brockman, the Brit named Andy said, "We think
they're liberal in Sweden, but its [*sic*] more like Northern England as
opposed to Southern Europe.

"In Monaco, Albert works 12 hours a day but at 9pm, when he goes out, he does whatever he wants, and nobody cares. But, if I do it, I'm in big trouble," the Brit said.

That is when, according to Brockman's own retelling, he "realized that the recipient of Irina's foot massage was his Royal Highness, Prince Andrew, the Duke of York." Prince Andrew has denied this encounter ever took place.

These are the sorts of stories that seem to follow Prince Andrew wherever he goes. In 2020 a local attorney general accused the British royal of groping women on Jeffrey Epstein's private island.[1]

"An employee told me that he saw Prince Andrew on a balcony out at Little St. James groping girls right out in the open," the U.S. Virgin Islands prosecutor Denise George said in an interview with *Vanity Fair*.[2]

"He said he remembered walking up to him and saying, 'Good morning, your Highness,'" the prosecutor said, retelling the conversation Prince Andrew had with Epstein's former employee.

—

Jeffrey Epstein was exposed. Getting investigated and arrested on child sex crimes revealed to him that he was vulnerable. Yes, he had effectively been able to minimize damage. Money, power, and friends in the right places helped. They always did.

But no matter how light the sentence he received, it was humiliating. It was also a hindrance—though not a complete one—to the three-a-day "massage" routine he demanded. Moreover, it came with various limitations: public shunning by some, like Bill Clinton, and being legally required to register as a sex offender.

It was what one might call a learning experience. Though to the public, Epstein was even less contrite. "I'm not a sexual predator, I'm an 'offender,'" he told the *New York Post* in a 2011 interview.

"It's the difference between a murderer and a person who steals a bagel," Epstein added.

He maintained that view until the end. "I just want you to know I'm not a pedophile," he told a Fox Business reporter in 2019.[3] "Maybe the only thing worse than being called a pedophile is being called a hedge fund manager."

Practically speaking, Epstein's new status as an admitted sex offender did not mean retreat for him. It did not mean a sudden change of behavior. Obviously not. No, it meant he had to get smarter, better, and more intentional.

"Jeffrey knew all of the right people in this game, and trading girls for favors is how he kept in the circle," one victim who accused Epstein of sex trafficking has claimed.

So he cozied up to his good friend Prince Andrew, the Duke of York, which would both help him re-ingratiate himself into the upper echelons of America's elite and provide a bit of protection from the prying eyes of a curious public and overzealous law enforcement officers.

"I remember when Andrew and Jeffrey Epstein first became friends," a source told *Vanity Fair*. "Jeffrey had Andrew put on a pair of sweatpants for the first time in his life. He had him wear blue jeans for the first time. It was Jeffrey who taught Andrew how to relax."

Relaxation—which, for the royal, allegedly came with a captive kid for his own sexual gratification—in exchange for what Epstein wanted.

—

Epstein and Prince Andrew had one thing in common: they both dated Ghislaine Maxwell. The shared love would seem unimaginable. A Brooklyn boy of Jewish heritage going out with the same woman once fancied by a British royal of unimpeachable lineage?

The connection might help explain the closeness of the trio, and also the weirdness.

"I met through his girlfriend back in 1999 who—and I'd known her since she was at university in the UK and it would be, to some extent, a stretch to say that as it were we were close friends," Prince Andrew said in a 2019 interview with the BBC, meant to deal with the fallout of his close relationship with Epstein.

In fact, a Maxwell friend revealed in an interview that the two were more than friends. Which might not have been the only fact that the British royal elided.

A letter in defense of Prince Andrew, by his private secretary, Alastair Watson, pegged the start of their relationship at least half a decade earlier. "The duke has known Mr Epstein since being introduced to him in the early 1990s. The insinuations and innuendos that have been made in relation to the duke are without foundation," Watson wrote in March 2011.

Regardless, Epstein and Prince Andrew were indisputably friends. "I saw him once or twice a year, perhaps maybe maximum of three times a year," the duke explained.

So close, indeed, that he'd usually stay at Epstein's house if it was vacant. "Quite often if I was in the United States and doing things and if he wasn't there, he would say, 'Well, why don't you come and use my

houses?' So I said, 'That's very kind, thank you very much indeed,'"
said the duke.

Indeed, he would at other times stay at Epstein's home—even if he
was in town. The duke claims to have admired Epstein solely for his
intellectual pursuits. "He had the most extraordinary ability to bring
extraordinary people together and that's the bit that I remember as
going to the dinner parties where you would meet academics, politicians, people from the United Nations, I mean it was a cosmopolitan
group of what I would describe as US eminents," he told the BBC.

The friendship wasn't just enjoyed in America. Epstein was a guest
of the duke's at Windsor Castle, and then they went on a shooting
expedition at Sandringham House, the queen's winter home, in 2000.

Andrew claims he had a keen awareness of the signs of child sex
abuse, because he was a patron of the U.K.'s National Society for the
Prevention of Cruelty to Children. "I knew what the things were to
look for but I never saw them," he said.

But in July 2006, a month after Epstein was arrested for the first
time in Palm Beach, Andrew invited him to his daughter Princess
Beatrice's eighteenth birthday party at Windsor Castle. "I'm afraid,
you see this is the problem is that an awful lot of this was going on in
the United States and I wasn't a party to it and I knew nothing about
it," he rather unconvincingly now claims.

Because it is now known that when Prince Andrew was aware of
Epstein's predilection for sexually abusing young girls, it did not prevent the royal from remaining friends with the pervert.

In December 2010, the duke came to New York and stayed at Epstein's mansion. Epstein was released from his sweetheart jail sentence
nearly a year and a half earlier, in July 2009.

—

Friendship was not the only thing binding Epstein and Prince Andrew together. There was also money.

In 2011, the British press revealed that the New York financier had helped the duke's ex-wife, Sarah Ferguson, the Duchess of York, with her enormous debts. She had accepted, through her assistant, around $20,000 (£15,000, to be exact) from Epstein.

The money was delivered in response to a direct appeal from Prince Andrew, the U.K. 's *Telegraph* reported in 2011.

"The convicted paedophile gave £15,000 to the Duchess's former personal assistant, Johnny O'Sullivan, after the Duke allegedly made a personal appeal to him to help his former wife with her financial troubles," the paper would write in a shocking exposé.

"The Duchess's spokesman confirmed last night that Epstein, who was sentenced to 18 months in jail for child sex offences in 2008, paid off part of the £78,000 the Duchess owed Mr O'Sullivan in a 'private arrangement' between the two men."

The astonishing thing is not so much that a British royal would take a rich financier's money; it's that a royal could be so cheaply bought.

Vanity Fair wrote that the real sum of money received by Ferguson was much, much larger. "The major reason Andrew hung out with Jeffrey was to get money for Sarah Ferguson," a source told the glossy magazine in a 2011 article.[4]

"Andrew feels responsible for Sarah. She walked away from their divorce with nothing, unlike Princess Diana, who got millions from Prince Charles. There have been newspaper reports that Sarah got £15,000 [$24,500] from Jeffrey, but I think that Sarah has actually received hundreds of thousands of dollars from him," the source claimed.

The Duchess of York was desperate. She was deeply in debt and needed cash. When she ended her marriage to the duke in 1996, she reportedly was in the hole £4.2 million.

The queen was reportedly "deeply concerned" about her ex-daughter-in-law's financial state. Bankruptcy by a royal, even an ex-royal, had never been claimed before. And it would be deeply humiliating for the entire family.

Despite being "continually on the verge of financial bankruptcy," as Ferguson once told Oprah, she has never had to file for bankruptcy. That's in part thanks to Epstein, and perhaps much more so than is even realized.[5]

Prince Andrew has been accused of sexual misconduct by Virginia Roberts Giuffre, who blames Maxwell for putting her in the situation.

On a visit to England in 2001, Maxwell awoke Giuffre one morning to say, "We're going shopping for a new ensemble . . . To go dancing with a Prince of England this evening," Giuffre has recalled in an unpublished book she shopped called "The Billionaire's Playboy Club."

"What . . . wow!" Giuffre replied, feigning interest and surprise.

All day they shopped as Maxwell prepped the girl for her forced date. "Make sure your [sic] bubbly and energetic, nobody want's [sic] a dead horse," Maxwell commanded. "Who knows where this could lead for you."

Giuffre, then seventeen, put on a pink mini-T-shirt to go with her embroidered jeans decorated with horses. She had a brand-new Burberry handbag to complement her outfit.

She was a nervous wreck. So she popped a Xanax to help keep her cool. Epstein and Maxwell both teased the kid for her nerves, she recalls.

Finally, at 6:00 p.m., Prince Andrew arrived. They exchanged kisses on the cheeks, and soon the three adults were shit-talking the royal's ex-wife, Sarah Ferguson.

The foursome then went to a nearby restaurant for dinner, where they were seated as couples—Jeffrey and Ghislaine on one side, Prince Andrew and Giuffre on the other. "I remained calm, cool, and collected, hoping that my nervousness wouldn't spill out at any given moment," Giuffre recalls.

Next the party traveled to the exclusive nightclub Tramp. Epstein took his usual place—a chair in the corner, where he could watch what would happen. Prince Andrew got everyone cocktails, except Epstein, whom he brought sparkling water, knowing full well that his friend didn't drink.

"I had the Prince's upmost attention. Moving his hands across the curves of my body, not to shy away from the fact that he was in public, he was whispering sweet nothings into my ear and kissing my neck. I would just giggle not really knowing how to reply to an aging man with a bad smile and terrible moves," she recalls. "He was the most incredibly hideous dancer I had ever seen."

The prince was dripping with sweat after an hour and wanted to go someplace quieter. They returned to Maxwell's house—as had been arranged. While back home, Giuffre and Prince Andrew posed for a photo that would one day become infamous when the *Daily Mail* published it in 2011. The smirking prince captured in a private home, with a provocative hand on the girl's bare midriff, which had been left exposed between her tiny pink top and her embroidered jeans.

Giuffre started a bath and seductively stripped her clothes, and they kissed as they entered the bath. "He was adorning my young body, particularly my feet, caressing my toes and licking my arches," Giuffre says, remembering that she laughed at the royal's apparent fetish.

"We dried off from the cold and retired to my bedchambers for the longest ten minutes of my life. Moments later and without any real emotional attachment, he burst in ecstasy, leaving me to my own feelings of dismay," she writes.[6]

Upon returning to the United States, Giuffre would be paid extra by Epstein for taking such good care of the prince. Though in private the two laughed at the royal's fetish.

Nevertheless, Giuffre felt enslaved. The money she earned would be spent on alcohol and pills, anything to help her mind feel less pain from the continuous experiences she could not escape.

Giuffre has claimed that the next day Ghislaine Maxwell, who herself once dated the duke, praised her for sexually gratifying the royal. "Ghislaine said, 'You did a really good job' and pats me on the back and says, 'You made him really happy,'" Giuffre has said.

This wouldn't be her only encounter with Prince Andrew; she recounts in detail another meetup in New York City at Epstein's home.

Prince Andrew denies all of Giuffre's claims, telling the BBC in 2019 he has "no recollection of ever meeting this lady, none whatsoever."[7]

His denials caused much snickering, especially in light of the photograph, which has long been released publicly. Prince Andrew concedes the man in the photo is indeed himself and stops short of saying that it's doctored, though he questioned whether that's his "hand" in the snap.

The royal claims that night he was with his children at Pizza Express, which he remembers nearly two decades later because it was such an "unusual thing" for him to do.

But the line that resulted in the most ridicule for the royal was this one: "There's a slight problem with the sweating because I have a peculiar medical condition which is that I don't sweat or I didn't sweat at the time."

It did not take long after Prince Andrew's sweating defense for photographic proof and testimonials to be published online that would undercut his denials.

—

A friend of Prince Andrew's has said that the royal defended his friendship with Epstein by claiming to be loyal.

"You cannot have a relationship with Jeffrey. You can't do these things," the friend claimed in a *Vanity Fair* interview that he told the duke after Epstein's guilty plea.

"Stop giving me a hard time. You're such a puritan," Prince Andrew reportedly told his friend.

A screaming match ensued, and finally Prince Andrew had had enough. "Leave me alone," the royal said in a huff. "Jeffrey's my friend. Being loyal to your friends is a virtue. And I'm going to be loyal to him."

But publicly, Prince Andrew tells a much different story. He maintains he visited Epstein in New York City to break up in 2010. "Look, you've been convicted, it would be incompatible for me to be seen with you," the duke claims to have told his buddy during a stroll through Central Park.

The problem with that version of events is that it seems implausible. The duke did not simply meet up with his buddy to deliver the devastating news. No, he once again slept at Epstein's New York City mansion, having a four-night slumber party instead of a perfunctory breakup, as if that were even needed.

"I could easily have gone and stayed somewhere else but sheer convenience of being able to get a hold of the man was . . . I mean he was in and out all over the place. So getting him in one place for a period of time to actually have a long enough conversation to say look, these are the reasons why I'm not going to . . . and that happened on the walk," Prince Andrew rather remarkably now claims.

The royal was "even spotted kissing a glammy brunette on the doorstep," the *New York Post* reported in 2011.[8]

It was on this visit that Epstein once again tried to use Prince Andrew for his own gain—to help him get back into the good graces of New York's media class. He threw a dinner party with Katie Couric, Charlie Rose, Woody Allen, Chelsea Handler, and George Stephanopoulos all in attendance. Two of those guests (Rose and Allen) would later face sexual misconduct allegations of their own. The group of under twenty guests would feast on lasagna. Epstein would entertain wearing his usual jeans, gussied up with $500 velvet Stubbs & Wootton slippers.

Epstein's longtime publicist, the New York socialite Peggy Siegal, facilitated the party, according to reports. "Multiple sources say the event was organized by Siegal, who presented it as an opportunity to meet the prince at the largest single-family dwelling in New York City. Given that it was less than two months after Kate Middleton and

Prince William's engagement, interest in the royals was running high," *The Hollywood Reporter* would explain.[9]

And yet it is a perfect example of Epstein's opportunism, using his high-profile friends to better his own standing—by bringing in high-profile media luminaries, who the press now claims were roped into the meeting under false pretenses.

The personal cost for Prince Andrew would be astronomical. A decade later, after Epstein's arrest and subsequent death, he'd be kicked out of Buckingham Palace by his mother, the queen of England.

"It has become clear to me over the last few days that the circumstances relating to my former association with Jeffrey Epstein has become a major disruption to my family's work and the valuable work going on in the many organisations and charities that I am proud to support," Prince Andrew said in a 2019 statement after his monumental BBC interview was so roundly roasted.[10] "I continue to unequivocally regret my ill-judged association with Jeffrey Epstein."

But no matter his relation to the royal family nor Epstein's death, it may not be over yet for Prince Andrew. Giuffre has been seeking justice through the American court system for years and will likely continue to do so. Even the FBI is hot on his heels.

In a bizarre and out-of-character move, American law enforcement authorities made a public plea, of sorts, to shame the British royal into cooperating with the investigation into Epstein. Indeed, the public statement was delivered practically on Epstein's stoop.

"The Southern District of New York and the FBI have contacted Prince Andrew's attorneys and requested to interview Prince Andrew, and to date, Prince Andrew has provided zero cooperation," the Manhattan U.S. attorney, Geoffrey Berman, intoned into the microphone at a press conference.[11]

The comment was obviously meant to shame the royal into cooperating—a pledge he'd made in that BBC interview. He "publicly offered, indeed in a press release, to cooperate with law enforcement investigating the crimes committed by Jeffrey Epstein and his co-conspirators," Berman said.

"Jeffrey Epstein couldn't have done what he did without the assistance of others," he added. "And I can assure you that the investigation is moving forward."

But for whatever reason Prince Andrew never appeared to be shamed. The public preaching fell on deaf ears. Perhaps it was because he knew Epstein could not speak from the grave. Others closer to home might not have been feeling so confident.

12

The Politician

Bill Clinton's Active Retirement

[He] had information on Bill Clinton & now he's dead. I see
#TrumpBodyCount trending but we know who did this!
A RETWEET FROM DONALD TRUMP, AUGUST 10, 2019[1]

Jeffrey Epstein was fascinated by Bill Clinton's Oval Office sex scandal. He told friends he was perplexed at why the president would throw away his reputation to carry on an affair with Monica Lewinsky, a woman who Epstein believed was too unattractive to sleep with. On a trip to Africa with Clinton, Epstein finally got his answer.

During the flight, while Clinton was still on the plane, one good friend remembers receiving a phone call from a highly amused Epstein. "Guess what I learned?" Epstein asked his somewhat befuddled friend, according to an interview.

"What?"

"I never understood the whole Monica Lewinsky thing, so I asked," said Epstein. "[Bill's] answer was, 'The government shutdown. She was the only girl at the White House!'"

Epstein's connections to the Clintons were long-standing and have been the source of intense speculation. Why did that powerful couple put up with Epstein despite his misdeeds?

The Clinton-Epstein connection first became known on September 21, 2002, when they traveled to Africa together. Flying high on Epstein's Boeing 727, along with Kevin Spacey and Chris Tucker, the two really got to know each other. They visited Ghana, Nigeria, Rwanda, Mozambique, and South Africa.

The 2002 trip would serve as a coming-out party of sorts for Epstein, resulting in Page Six items in the *New York Post* and a monster puff piece in *New York* magazine. Titled "Jeffrey Epstein: International Moneyman of Mystery," the *New York* article by Landon Thomas Jr. asked, "Who in the world is Jeffrey Epstein?"[2] The question was asked because, well, no one really knew who this guy was.

The article would be a seminal piece—defining him by his money, access, and predilection for young women. It was there where Donald Trump made his now infamous quotation stating, "I've known Jeff for fifteen years. Terrific guy . . . He's a lot of fun to be with. It is even said that he likes beautiful women as much as I do, and many of them are on the younger side. No doubt about it—Jeffrey enjoys his social life."

Of course that aspect of his life would go unexplored for years to come. Instead, the focus at the time would be on his profession and his big heart. (Both things the author would basically get wrong.)

"What attracted Clinton to Epstein was quite simple: He had a plane (he has a couple, in fact—the Boeing 727, in which he took Clinton to Africa, and, for shorter jaunts, a black Gulfstream, a Cessna 421, and a helicopter to ferry him from his island to St. Thomas). Clinton had organized a weeklong tour of South Africa, Nigeria, Ghana, Rwanda, and Mozambique to do what Clinton does. So when the president's advance man Doug Band pitched the idea to Epstein, he said sure. As an added bonus, Kevin Spacey, a close friend of Clinton's, and actor Chris Tucker came along for the ride," the article stated.

"While Epstein got an intellectual kick out of engaging African finance ministers in theoretical chitchat about economic development, the real payoff for him was observing Clinton in his métier: talking HIV/aids policy with African leaders and soaking up the love from Cape Town to Lagos."

—

When Bill Clinton left the White House, he did so as a broken man. Though he remained popular, he was an impeached ex-president who had, by some measures, squandered his credibility as leader of the free world by chasing a young intern, instead of focusing on the policy platform that got him elected and then reelected by historically slim margins.

At fifty-four years old, Clinton was still young. He was not ready to retire to the golf course or stay home alone as his wife, Hillary Rodham Clinton, served the people of New York as its junior senator. But he was also toxic.

The 2000 election was deeply humiliating—and not solely because his vice president, Al Gore, lost in a direct rebuke to Clinton and his impeachment. Worse, Clinton was not wanted on the campaign trail. The master politician who had redefined the Democratic Party was a pariah. Few wanted to be seen with him or near him. And that was before his last-minute pardons of family and friends that Republicans would savage for years to come.

Clinton was depressed for the first few months after moving to Chappaqua, New York. He was living outside government housing for the first time in nearly two decades. Restoring his image was his top priority, and so he focused his attention on his presidential library, the Clinton Foundation, and later the Clinton Global Initiative. But he also focused on getting paid.

He was, after all, broke. The legal bills he faced from the impeachment process landed him millions of dollars in debt, and he needed to pay up. His position was made more difficult by the fact that he lost his law license as a result of a settlement he reached on the sexual harassment claim levied against him by Paula Jones.

Privately, he also worried about building up enough money to take care of his family's legacy. Men in Clinton's family tended to die young, and he worried he would follow this trend.

"The next two or three years, I want to spend roughly half my time making money," Clinton told his longtime friend Taylor Branch during one of their last conversations at the White House on January 8, 2001.[3] "I'm coming off two terms, a two-term presidency with high public ratings, and rating still rising, and contacts all over the world . . . I know where to find this money, I think I can find it, so that's what I want to do."

So he sought opportunity—and people—who could help solve his problems. Enter Jeffrey Epstein.

Epstein's early forays into politics coincided with the rise of Clinton's political star. In the 1992 election cycle, he gave $2,000 to the charismatic young Arkansas governor in his successful effort to unseat

George H. W. Bush, according to federal election disclosure records. But he also gave $1,000 to Bush, perhaps a sign that he was not as interested in ideology as he was in access.

John Glenn, the Democratic senator from Ohio, received decent donations too. On one of those $1,000 donations Epstein listed his employer as Limited Inc., one of the brands owned by his friend and patron, Leslie Wexner.

He also gave to Bob Packwood, where he listed his employer as Wexner Investments. Packwood, a Republican senator from Oregon, would soon resign his Senate seat in the wake of detailed sexual assault and harassment allegations. Epstein would also give to Eliot Spitzer, though much later, who as governor of New York would resign after it was revealed he had frequented high-end prostitutes.

In sum, Epstein is believed to have given $184,276 directly to politicians, with a heavy lean toward Democrats ($147,426 versus $18,250 to Republicans, with the rest going to independents).[4] Many hundreds of thousands more went to other party functions and fundraisers.

With the slew of donations, access came easily. Around 1993, Epstein donated $10,000 to the White House Historical Association, contributing to the Clintons' efforts to redecorate the residence with gold drapes and other lavish decor. In return, Epstein received a perfunctory thank-you letter from the association and an invitation to a donor reception with the Clintons. He brought Ghislaine Maxwell as his date, according to White House records obtained by the *Daily Beast*. That reception was the first known meeting between Epstein, Maxwell, and the Clintons.[5]

But his real introduction to Clinton, according to one of Epstein's former lawyers, was through Lynn Forester, a striking blond telecom executive and New York socialite who later married into the Rothschild family. Forester was in her early forties at the time and newly divorced from her second husband, the New York City councilman Andrew Stein. She was smitten with Epstein and became an evangelist for his financial services, introducing him to her elite circle of friends.

So it was no surprise that when Forester had a chance to talk to Clinton during a dinner at Senator Ted Kennedy's house in 1995, the two ended up chatting about Epstein instead of the social policy she had intended to discuss.

"It was a pleasure to see you," Forester told Clinton in a 1995 letter.[6] "Using my fifteen seconds of access to discuss Jeffrey Epstein and currency stabilization, I neglected to talk to you about a topic near and dear to my heart. Namely, affirmative action and the future." Clearly she thought enough of Epstein to relegate her personal "near and dear" topics to the follow-up, rather than the actual conversation, in order to sing his praises.

Epstein was also cultivating other members of Clinton's inner circle around the same time. Also in 1995, a dinner was held at the Palm Beach home of Ron Perelman, the billionaire investor behind the cosmetics giant Revlon. It was a three-hour intimate affair, *The Palm Beach Post* reported at the time.[7] Jeffrey Epstein was in attendance along with Jimmy Buffett, Clinton's college friend Arnold Paul Prosperi, and Diandra Douglas, who was then married to the actor Michael Douglas. The cost to get in: a $100,000 donation to the Democratic National Committee. The New York financier would also visit an aide to Clinton multiple times at the White House, the *Daily Beast* would later report.

After Clinton left the White House, the ex-president's relationship with Epstein would grow much, much closer. For Clinton, Epstein had it all. Money, power, and his own fleet of airplanes. Plus the helicopter (used to reach his private island) and many, many vehicles. The former president had another ulterior interest in befriending Epstein, but that wouldn't become clear to Clinton's inner circle until later.

So they took their relationship to the next level. They began hanging out together and traveling.

Flight logs indicate that Clinton flew from Miami to Westchester, New York, on February 9, 2002, with Epstein. The logs further reveal Clinton traveled from New York to London on March 19, 2002. He returned home March 21, 2002. He also traveled May 22, 2002, from Japan to Hong Kong. On May 23, he flew to Singapore, leaving May 24 for Bangkok. On July 12, 2002, he and his daughter, Chelsea, attended the royal wedding of King Mohammed VI with Lalla Salma in Rabat, Morocco. On July 13, 2002, he flew home to New York, with a brief stop in the Azores.[8]

Traveling with Clinton gave Epstein both joy and frustration. In some ways they shared personality traits. Neither had the capacity to form truly close friendships, according to those who knew them. They also tended to use other people as a means to an end.

As one New York journalist told the author Carol Felsenthal about Epstein, "He's truly a brilliant autodidact, but sort of crippled in a personal sense and who does that remind you of?"[9]

The answer to that rhetorical question was obvious—Bill Clinton. The similarities were very real. Both had an impressive and innate ability to wow their audiences, with little preparation. They were both also highly motivated by sex.

—

Although the closeness of various politicos and Epstein remains some-thing of a mystery to this day—Bill Richardson, for instance, is not keen to divulge the details of his Epstein relationship—one thing was always central in nearly all of Epstein's relationships: money. Epstein had it; the politicians wanted it.

But what the politicians could offer was legitimacy. Public state-ments of praise from a well-respected politician can help private-sector businessmen ingratiate themselves with clients or other well-heeled moneymen throughout the world.

Which is perhaps why Bill Clinton offered his own public praise for his then friend—after going on a free trip to Africa in the early 2000s. "Jeffrey is both a highly successful financier and a com-mitted philanthropist with a keen sense of global markets and an in-depth knowledge of twenty-first-century science. I especially ap-preciated his insights and generosity during the recent trip to Africa to work on democratization, empowering the poor, citizen service, and combating HIV/AIDS," Clinton would tell *New York* maga-zine.[10]

But the secret was, Epstein did not actually like Clinton. Nor did Clinton like Epstein. There were signs of tension from their first trip to Europe in 2002. Epstein's pilot David Rodgers said the flight crew had barely checked into the hotel when he "got word from Secret Service that President Clinton wanted to leave that night."

"When we went there we thought we were going to be there for likely probably at least a couple of nights. But it didn't turn out—we didn't even spend one night there," Rodgers said in a videotaped depo-sition.

It's unclear why Clinton felt such an urgency to leave London. Epstein continued to take the former president on other overseas plane trips, but Clinton's personality soon started to grate on him.

Upon returning from the trip to Africa, Epstein further confided in one good friend, "Boy, that was a mistake."

"Why?" asked the friend.

"I don't like the guy," Epstein told him at the time.

Epstein claimed he did not like Clinton because he did not think he was a good person, the friend recounted. "He just didn't respect him; he was all over how horrible of a person he was," the friend recalled in an interview.

But in truth the verdict might have been more mixed. "If you were a boxer at the downtown gymnasium at 14th Street and Mike Tyson walked in, your face would have the same look as these foreign leaders had when Clinton entered the room. He is the world's greatest politician," he reportedly told another friend.[11]

Despite Epstein's apparent mixed views of Clinton, the relationship continued after the Africa sojourn. Epstein seemed to have the president's ear whenever he wanted it, according to confidants.

Alan Dershowitz, the Harvard professor and criminal defense attorney, vividly remembers a summer dinner at Caroline Kennedy's Martha's Vineyard home in the late 1990s with Bill and Hillary Clinton.

"Before dinner we were standing around having cocktails. A Secret Service agent came over to President Clinton and gave him the phone and said someone wants to talk to you," Dershowitz recalled in an interview.

"[Clinton] went off for five, maybe ten minutes, had a conversation. Then he came back and said, 'Alan, somebody wants to talk to you.' He gave me his phone, and it was Jeffrey Epstein. I said, 'What are you doing on the phone?' He said 'Oh, I'm talking to Bill.' That was it. Of course, there's no question he had a friendship with Bill Clinton," said Dershowitz.

The Africa trip would also prove to be a fatal mistake for Epstein. The public praise would, in the long run, be to his detriment. The question is, what reason did he have for keeping Clinton around in the meanwhile? And what was Clinton getting out of Epstein?

—

Clinton was allegedly carrying on an affair with at least one woman in Epstein's orbit, but she was well over the age of consent.

Ghislaine Maxwell, a constant presence at the ex-president's side during these trips, was the primary reason Clinton let Epstein ferry him around the world.

"[Bill] and Ghislaine were getting it on," a source who witnessed the relationship said in an interview. "That's why he was around Epstein— to be with her."

The source explained that reporters have been missing the point about the Clinton-Epstein relationship by focusing on Epstein's sex crimes. "[Clinton's] stupid but not an idiot," the source says, dismissing the idea that the ex-president was sexually involved with children.

Clinton's primary interest in Epstein was the woman he once dated and who allegedly helped procure her ex-boyfriend's future victims.

"You couldn't hang out with her without being with him," the source said of the Epstein-Clinton relationship.

"Clinton just used him like everything else," the source explains. In this case, Epstein was being used as an alibi while he hooked up with Maxwell.

The relationship between Clinton and Maxwell was not confined to these overseas junkets. It continued in New York City, where Clinton on multiple occasions visited Maxwell's own private townhome at 116 East Sixty-fifth Street, an $11 million pad that runs a touch below seven thousand square feet, much more modest than Epstein's palatial townhome a few blocks north. (Maxwell purchased it in 2000 for a mere $4.95 million.)

The coziness between the former president and the charming British socialite drew notice in New York social circles. Clinton and Maxwell were spotted dining together at the Madison Avenue Italian mainstay Nello, according to a 2002 *New York* magazine article, which described Maxwell as a "man-eater" in the same paragraph. When Clinton went stag to a New York education charity gala in late 2001—Hillary declined to attend—Maxwell was reportedly at his side.

The relationship also carried over to the Clinton Global Initiative and Clinton Foundation. Maxwell became somewhat of a fixture at these events. It was there where she was even served court papers about her participation in Epstein's abuse.

On July 31, 2010 Maxwell was among the few guests to attend Chelsea Clinton's wedding at the former Astor estate in Rhinebeck, New York. This auspicious event followed an embarrassing incident for Maxwell.

"Only a few months earlier, while attending the Clinton Global Initiative in New York City, at the end of an Indian summer, in

September 2009, a process server walked through the packed lobby of the Sheraton Hotel on Eighth Avenue . . . and served Ghislaine Maxwell papers for a deposition," the journalist Conchita Sarnoff recalls.

"Maxwell . . . was huddled in a small group talking to other guests" as the server approached her. He "called out her name and . . . with so many people surrounding her, Maxwell was unsuspecting. She confirmed her identity and he served her notice. The deposition was in relation to Epstein's sexual abuse case. The server left at once," Sarnoff writes in her book, *TrafficKing*.[12]

"Ironically, photographs of Maxwell taken by a private investigator who accompanied the process server showed Maxwell receiving notice while standing beneath a human trafficking banner. Human trafficking was the Conference's theme at the 2009 Clinton Global Initiative," she writes.

"Maxwell never appeared at the deposition claiming, the day prior to her testimony she had to immediately return to England to care for her dying mother. At the time of that trip, . . . the elder Mrs. Maxwell was not gravely ill. Not long after the deposition was scheduled, Maxwell was spotted again in New York. As a British subject there was nothing the attorneys could do to force her to take the deposition."

Clinton, though he has a long history of being accused of sexual misconduct, has never been accused of engaging with an underage female with Epstein. Despite rampant speculation, in fact Clinton's appetite was being fed by someone else entirely.

"I have seen reports saying or implying that I had sex with former president Bill Clinton on Little Saint James Island," Giuffre has said in court documents. "Former president Bill Clinton was present on the island at a time when I was also present on the island, but I have never had sexual relations with Clinton, nor have I ever claimed to have such relations. I have never seen him have sexual relations with anyone."

This apparently wasn't for lack of trying by Epstein. After returning from his trip to Asia with Bill Clinton, Epstein boasted that he had tried to rope Clinton into a hotel room orgy with him, a bevy of young women, and Mick Jagger of the Rolling Stones.

"He said that he flew with Clinton," said Dershowitz in an interview. "When they landed in Asia . . . Mick Jagger had a party in his room with lots of young women and lots of sex, like an orgy.

"Epstein was there, and Clinton walked in and saw what was going on, immediately said, 'No, no, no, this is not my thing,' and walked out. Epstein told me that story," said Dershowitz. "Obviously, there were lots of people there, and whatever Clinton did, he didn't do it in public."

But involvement with Maxwell herself raises serious questions. After all, Maxwell isn't just a former lover of Epstein's. She is an alleged co-conspirator in Epstein's sex crimes.

During the same time period when she was close with Clinton, Maxwell was allegedly recruiting underage women to engage in paid sex acts with Epstein, according to court testimony from multiple alleged victims.

"Maxwell was heavily involved in the illegal sex," Giuffre has also said in court documents. "I understood her to be a very powerful person. She used Epstein's money and he used her name and connections to gain power and prestige."

Additionally, Giuffre has said in legal documents, "One way to describe Maxwell's role was as the 'madame.' She assumed a position of trust for all the girls, including me. She got me to trust her and Epstein. It turned out that Maxwell was all about sex all the time. She had sex with underaged girls virtually every day when I was around her, and she was very forceful."

Giuffre has detailed their sexual interactions at the Palm Beach mansion, the Virgin Islands residence, the New Mexico ranch, the New York townhome, France, and "many other locations." The victim has said, "I also observed Maxwell have sex with dozens of underage girls."

Johanna Sjoberg, a woman who says Maxwell recruited her when she was a student at Palm Beach Atlantic University, claimed the British media heiress punished her for failing to make Epstein reach orgasm during one session.

"[Ghislaine] called me after I had left and said, I have the camera [I bought] for you, but you cannot receive it yet because you came here and didn't finish your job and I had to finish it for you," said Sjoberg. "She was implying that I did not get Jeffrey off, and so she had to do it."[13]

In one of the most disturbing accounts, Maxwell allegedly confiscated the passport and cell phone of a fifteen-year-old Swedish girl who was pressured to have sex with Maxwell on Epstein's private island, according to court testimony from a former house manager for Epstein's friends Eva and Glenn Dubin.

Rinaldo Rizzo, the former house manager for Epstein's friends Eva and Glenn Dubin, has said he saw indications that something was off when he visited Epstein's house for a pool party.

"As I'm walking to the bathroom, what caught my eye, and I had to take a double look, there were pictures of naked women, half-dressed girls," said Rizzo in a deposition. "I leaned over and started looking at these pictures for a brief minute, and it was just so coincidental that as I did that, Ms. Maxwell enters, and she immediately says to me that Jeffrey would like for me to rejoin the party immediately."

—

Alfredo Rodriguez, a former butler for Epstein, also said Maxwell kept nude photographs of young girls on her computer that appeared to be surreptitiously taken.

"I don't think they knew they were being photographed," said Rodriguez in a court deposition.

But never mind the accusations. They did not appear to bother the Clintons. In fact, even after the court documents detailing the worst of her alleged crimes, the former first family was still keen to have Maxwell hang around.

She vacationed with Chelsea Clinton. And she was at Chelsea's wedding to the son of the ex-congressman Edward Mezvinsky and ex-congresswoman Marjorie Margolies, Marc Mezvinsky.

A source with knowledge of the situation says that Chelsea Clinton's connection continually brought Maxwell closer to the former first family.

"Chelsea vacationed with her and kept her around the foundation," the source said in an interview. "She went to her wedding!"

Other reporters have touched on the same detail. "Ghislaine was the contact between Epstein and Clinton," *Politico* quoted a source as saying. "She ended up being close to the family because she and Chelsea ended up becoming close."

Chelsea Clinton's chief of staff, Bari Lurie, has denied the coziness of the relationship. "It wasn't until 2015 that Chelsea and (her husband) Marc became aware of the horrific allegations against Ghislaine Maxwell and hope that all the victims find justice," Lurie said to *Politico* in a statement. "Chelsea and Marc were friendly with her because of her relationship with a dear friend of theirs. When that relationship ended, Chelsea and Marc's friendship with her ended as well."[14]

All this despite the volumes of legal documents filed against Epstein and his alleged madam, Maxwell.

And her parents have also denied having knowledge of Epstein's alleged sex crimes, beyond what's been published in news reports.

"President Clinton knows nothing about the terrible crimes Jeffrey Epstein pleaded guilty to in Florida some years ago, or those with which he has been recently charged in New York," his spokesman Angel Ureña said in a statement shortly after Epstein's 2019 arrest.

"In 2002 and 2003, President Clinton took a total of four trips on Jeffrey Epstein's airplane: one to Europe, one to Asia, and two to Africa, which included stops in connection with the work of the Clinton Foundation. Staff, supporters of the Foundation, and his Secret Service detail traveled on every leg of every trip. He had one meeting with Epstein in his Harlem office in 2002, and around the same time made one brief visit to Epstein's New York apartment with a staff member and his security detail. He's not spoken to Epstein in well over a decade, and has never been to Little St. James Island, Epstein's ranch in New Mexico, or his residence in Florida."[15]

The last known flight Clinton took aboard Epstein's jet was November 4, 2003, flying from Brussels to Oslo, for an HIV/AIDS project, and then flying to Hong Kong, Siberia, and Beijing.

▬

After Epstein pleaded guilty to sex crimes in 2008, Maxwell had to strike out on her own. Much like Clinton, who had left the White House under a dark cloud, she had to hatch a plan to be welcomed back to polite society. And she did it with the assistance of none other than the Clintons.

Maxwell did what conscientious liberals do and in 2012 built a charitable organization around a do-gooder pet cause. She created the TerraMar Project, a nonprofit focusing on conserving the world's oceans. She credited her interest in the project with once finding a plastic hanger on the ocean floor, but her love of yachting might have been just as important.

For Maxwell, big boats—and access to them—were a status symbol she appeared to relish. She would reportedly brag about Jeffrey Epstein's client Les Wexner's yacht as though it were her own.

"Ghislaine would always call me and say, 'I'm coming down to use the boat with some friends.' I would always tell her, 'I have to call the owner. I can't just let you on the boat.' And she would never show up," the former captain of Wexner's yacht, Craig Tafoya, told *The New York Times*. "She did that half a dozen times. And in talking to a guy who worked for [the yacht's designer], he said, 'She does that all the time. She does it when she's in front of all her girlfriends and wants to brag that she can go use someone's yacht.'"[16]

Whatever had prompted her to start it, the TerraMar Project gave

Maxwell an avenue to re-ingratiate herself into polite society. She began giving interviews, making public speeches, and of course making pitches at charitable gatherings, like the Clinton Global Initiative.

At a 2013 Clinton Global Initiative meeting in New York City, the TerraMar Project was able to secure commitments from participants to help "mobilize the international community and the public at large on the importance of the Oceans and the Seas."[17] Of course, four years earlier Maxwell had been subpoenaed for alleged participation in Epstein's sex crimes at that very same conference.

But reports indicate that Epstein was the original funder of the Clinton Global Initiative. Though the Clintons have not confirmed this, it's been written that Epstein gave Bill Clinton's pet project $4 million to get off the ground.

Tax records reveal little about TerraMar's activities, though they do show that Maxwell wasn't able to raise enough funds to run the nonprofit without incurring debt.

—

Ironically, in some ways it took Hillary Clinton losing the 2016 presidential election for Epstein to finally be brought to justice.

In the years after Donald Trump won his presidential election in 2016, media exposés would chronicle vivid stories of rampant sexual abuse across America. Hollywood celebrities, business executives, and politicians would be embarrassed and brought down.[18] It was called the #MeToo movement, and it exposed men who used status and power to dominate, and violate, women.

The media wrote about a reckoning in American culture. The idea being that the behavior of old would no longer be tolerated. That imbalance of power, male dominance, and sexual assault were out. Respect for the victims and the right for their stories to be heard and believed were in.

There were some clear outliers. Bill Clinton, who himself had been accused of sexual assault in the past, did not see his behavior reexamined amid our new enlightenment. The current president, Donald Trump, also had many of his own accusations; though Democrats tended to hold these charges against him, Republicans by and large gave him a pass.

Epstein had ties to both. For Clinton, the two had struck up a friendship going back as far as the early 1990s, meeting at the White House on at least several occasions. That was only the beginning. As an ex-president, the friendship flourished, with Clinton joining Epstein on his private jet, sickeningly dubbed the Lolita Express, after Vladimir Nabokov's novel *Lolita* about a middle-aged man's obsession and love of a twelve-year-old girl, for round-the-world jaunts.

Trump, well before he ran for president as a Republican, attended events with Epstein in Palm Beach and Manhattan, where both had homes. Then a real estate mogul who had flirted with presidential politics with a half-assed third-party run in 1999, he appeared well aware of his acquaintance's criminal proclivities. Trump would later claim to have banned his associate from Mar-a-Lago, his Palm Beach resort,[19] for making unwelcome sexual advances, though *The New York Times* would report that the fallout was instead over business disagreements.[20]

In fact, a clear line can be drawn from the 2016 election of Trump and the #MeToo movement, when the accusations levied against the president caused some in the media and the Democratic Party to reexamine their own relationship with sexual predators. And of course there's a clear connection between the #MeToo movement and the reexamination of Jeffrey Epstein.

The supposed financier had run afoul of the law before. In 2008, Epstein had pleaded guilty to procuring an underage girl for prostitution. His admission gave him tremendous leniency in sentencing, allowing him to work out a special thirteen-month custody arrangement that permitted him to leave state lockup daily to go to work.

The prosecutor who granted such a sweet deal was none other than Alex Acosta, who would be nominated as secretary of the Department of Labor in February 2017 and confirmed by the full Senate in April of that year, with a bipartisan 60–38 vote. Acosta had reportedly claimed to the Trump administration when he was interviewing to be secretary of labor that he couldn't bring down the hammer on Epstein because he was an asset to the intelligence community. "I was told Epstein 'belonged to intelligence' and to leave it alone," Acosta revealed to the White House.[21]

Acosta's rise to such a high-profile cabinet-level job led at least one paper to look into the leniency of the original deal with the sexual predator. The explosive and infuriating investigation opened with an article in the *Miami Herald* with the damning headline "How a Future Trump Cabinet Member Gave a Serial Sex Abuser the Deal of a Lifetime."[22]

Acosta, the article alleged, had made the Epstein deal with a lawyer representing the predator, Jay Lefkowitz, a former George W. Bush administration official then working at the highly regarded Kirkland & Ellis law firm. The two lawyers met at unconventional locations—more appropriate for friends catching up than opposing counsels duking it out. The end result was a joke of a sentence, a plea agreement that wouldn't disclose the number of accusers. More shocking still was that Epstein's co-conspirators were granted immunity and the victims were prevented from even learning about the deal, the *Herald* reporting alleged.

The series of stories, called "Perversion of Justice," yanked the spotlight right back onto Epstein and his wealthy and powerful protectors. The renewed focus and subsequent fallout were nearly immediate. The lead journalist on the story, Julie K. Brown, had done impressive work tracking down victims and presented it in a captivating manner.

Public outcry was swift and powerful. At a time when debates over inequality already dominated the public discourse, here was yet another example that there was one set of rules for the wealthy and privileged and another set for everyone else. And this time the wealthy villains weren't just getting away with hiding their cash or profiting off someone else's economic misfortune. Jeffrey Epstein was accused of some of the most disgusting offenses in the criminal code, and plenty of people helped him get away with it.

This story even managed to transcend the traditional polarized boundaries of American outrage. The condemnation was bipartisan. Democrats and Republicans were furious. Law enforcement was reengaged, and finally the jig was up.

Epstein was arrested again on July 6, 2019, as he stepped off his private jet in Teterboro Airport in New Jersey. The charges were (again) horrific—sex trafficking of minors a decade and a half earlier. Prosecutors said the evidence was solid. They had also recovered what amounted to child pornography, nude snaps of his victims. Stories swirled, with public reports suggesting that the alleged human trafficking ring was huge, international, and beyond the scope of what anyone had ever imagined.

More destructive to Americans' trust in public institutions was all Epstein's high-profile friends. If Trump had publicly acknowledged awareness of Epstein's proclivity for having sex with girls "on the younger side"—that is, underage—didn't that mean that his other elite pals had to know what was going on?

It was not just Epstein who would feel the heat. A week after the arrest, on July 12, Acosta would resign amid outrage over his decade-old plea deal. "The work release was complete BS," Acosta admitted in a press conference, a failed attempt to alleviate the mounting political pressure, two days before his resignation.[23]

"We believe we proceeded appropriately," he added. "We did what we did because we wanted to see Epstein go to jail."

———

After Epstein's death, Ghislaine Maxwell practically disappeared. In the weeks following his death, there was a mad dash to find her. No one did.

That is until she showed up in the New York Post in a seemingly staged photograph at an In-N-Out fast-food restaurant in Los Angeles.[24] The paper claimed, "Maxwell, 57, the alleged madam to the multimillionaire pedophile, was scarfing down a burger, fries and shake al fresco at an In-N-Out Burger on Monday while reading 'The Book of Honor: The Secret Lives and Deaths of CIA Operatives,' a nonfiction best-seller by journalist Ted Gup."

The book—and makeup-free photo of the usually glamorous Maxwell in a bluish-gray lightweight hoodie—would be a bit too pat. But regardless, that would be, as of this writing, the last time she was seen in public. Her name would be mentioned. She would, in the absence of Epstein, face civil legal actions, including a defamation lawsuit filed by Giuffre.

"Well, I guess this is the last time I'll be eating here!" she told a fellow diner. There were rumors she was hiding out with a boyfriend in New England or that she was sailing the high seas. But wherever she was, she couldn't be found.

Privately, she seemed somewhat relieved that Epstein was gone, her friend Laura Goldman told us.

"You know, it may be for the best," she said, according to Goldman's account of a phone call they had shortly after Epstein died.

On March 18, 2020, Ghislaine sued Epstein's estate for legal and private security fees. In the lawsuit, filed in the U.S. Virgin Islands, she said Epstein had promised in 2004 that he would always support her financially. Meanwhile, many speculated that her old flame Bill Clinton was involved in Epstein's death, perhaps because the Clintons feared he would reveal their secrets.

Even President Donald Trump helped fan the flames. Hours after news broke, a Twitter user under the handle @w_terrence tweeted a message:[25]

Died of SUICIDE on 24/7 SUICIDE WATCH ? Yeah right! How does that happen
#JefferyEpstein had information on Bill Clinton & now he's dead
I see #TrumpBodyCount trending but we know who did this!

RT if you're not Surprised

#EpsteinSuicide #ClintonBodyCount #ClintonCrimeFamily

The message, accompanied by a short video expounding on the theory, was retweeted by the president of the United States. Immediately the press pounced, complaining once again that Trump was quick to spread unverified, conspiratorial messages.

But Trump, as per usual, refused to cave. "The retweet—which is what it was, just a retweet—was from somebody that's a very respected conservative pundit, so I think that was fine," Trump said days later. He did, however, claim to have "no idea" if in fact the Clintons were involved.

"I know he was on his plane 27 times, and he said he was on the plane four times," Trump told the press of Clinton and Epstein. "But when they checked the plane logs, Bill Clinton—who was a very good friend of Epstein—he was on the plane about 27 or 28 times. So why did he say four times?"

The comment was a reference to Clinton's apparently downplaying his association with Epstein.

Trump, whose own relationship with Epstein reportedly deteriorated after the fellow Palm Beach resident made a pass at a young girl at his Mar-a-Lago club, further poured gas on the conspiracy.

"The question you have to ask is, did Bill Clinton go to the island? Because Epstein had an island. That was not a good place, as I understand it, and I was never there," Trump told the press. "So you have to ask, did Bill Clinton go to the island? That's the question. If you find that out, you're going to know a lot."[26]

Clinton's own spokesman Angel Ureña responded to Trump's tweet by calling for his removal. "Ridiculous, and of course not true—and Donald Trump knows it. Has he triggered the 25th Amendment yet?" he said on Twitter expressing outrage.[27]

Ureña had previously told the press, "President Clinton knows nothing about the terrible crimes Jeffrey Epstein pleaded guilty to in Florida some years ago, or those with which he has been recently charged in New York."[28]

13
Epstein's Secret

The Wexner Connection

*During the interview Epstein told her to undress and actually
assisted her to do so while saying, "Let me manhandle you for a
second."*

SANTA MONICA POLICE DEPARTMENT

Undoubtedly, many in powerful positions are happy that their
sexual peccadilloes are not being talked about in a court of law,
splashed across tabloids, mocked incessantly on social media.
Those would have been some of the consequences if Jeffrey Epstein
had decided to seek retribution after his second arrest. But there's another glaring mystery that has perplexed those observing the case:
Where exactly did Epstein's money come from?

There has always been wild speculation about the sources of Epstein's income. Did he blackmail the rich and famous, forcing countless exchanges of millions of dollars so that he would not release sex
tapes of them getting it on with his harem of young girls? Did he simply charge a fee, so to speak, to traffic children for sexual abuse, rack-
ing up large sums of money from high-dollar clients around the world?

Did he launder money for some of the world's most hardened criminals and accumulate so much in commissions and fees that he too
became über-wealthy?

Or was his own purported business as a money manager to billionaires successful enough that eventually he was able to join their
ranks?

All of these are possibilities, of course. Or in the end it was some
combination of all these schemes—plus more—that helped account
for Epstein's wealth.

Here's what we do know for sure: Epstein was said to be worth
more than $500 million at the time of his death, yet despite all the
press reports, despite all the scrutiny, only one single major client of
Jeffrey Epstein has ever been confirmed. His name is Leslie Wexner,
the multibillionaire founder of the clothing giant L Brands, owner of
the clothier the Limited and the lingerie giant Victoria's Secret, and
one of Epstein's first big clients.

"He told me he had five clients, each worth over a billion dollars,
and that he didn't take clients worth less than a billion dollars," said
Dershowitz. "That he was very good at understanding the tax ramifi-
cations and that he would never handle my money or money for people like me because we were not rich enough."

The amount of money that is known that Epstein got from Wexner
is alone enough to account for his $500 million final net worth upon
his death. At least in theory.

But to call Epstein solely a money manager is a mistake. "This idea
that, that somehow there are clients out there that he did things for—
you know, financial advisory services—that's just a fiction; that's just a
cover story. In my view, he provided services, but they had nothing to

do with financial services. He wasn't qualified to provide financial services," said one plugged-in former Wall Streeter in an interview.

Laura Goldman, Maxwell's friend, said she occasionally tried to talk to Epstein about investments when they saw each other at parties in the 1990s but found him to be cagey about his work.

"He was rumored to be an excellent manager," she said. "When you asked him questions, he didn't really want to discuss it. I would always get the feeling, why doesn't this person want to discuss this? My feeling, it was kind of odd."

Some, however, appreciated the financial advice he would sometimes pass down. "You know, he was a good guy, he did a hundred things for me," a friend of his said in an interview. "He called me in the office in 2008 to say sell all your stock now. No one made him do that. And how he knew that the market was going to crash, I couldn't tell you. But he sure as hell knew."

And yet Goldman, a former stockbroker, said she has never met anyone who traded with Epstein.

"I went to Wharton in the go-go years, when Wall Street was where everything came from, and everybody I went to school with, not one person knew anybody who traded with Epstein," she said. "How could that be?"

Goldman suspects that Epstein was not doing much investing, but was actually parking money in various places to mitigate Wexner's losses and liabilities.

"I don't think on any level he was a brilliant investor," she said.

But Epstein did have one remarkable ability that helped him sink his hooks firmly into Wexner's life, according to Epstein's former boss and convicted Ponzi scammer Steven Hoffenberg.

"He could really interpret weaknesses," said Hoffenberg. "He was the best seducer of people, the biggest manipulator I ever saw."

—

The relationship between Epstein and Wexner might have been the most important to Epstein's life. It is likely responsible for his biggest financial windfall ever, paving the way for him to own some of the most luxurious properties in the world, as well as his own airplane.

It is easy to imagine that Epstein would have been wealthy and successful without ever meeting Wexner, given his quick ascension from college dropout to Bear Stearns partner in 1980. But it is unlikely that he himself would ever have joined the ranks of the über-rich without Wexner's assistance.

"I first met Mr. Epstein in the mid-1980s, through friends who vouched for and recommended him as a knowledgeable financial professional," Wexner stated in 2019, trying to deflect criticism of his relations with Epstein by claiming unnamed others made the connection.[1]

"Mr. Epstein represented that he had various well-known and respected individuals both as his financial clients and in his inner circle. Based on positive reports from several friends, and on my initial dealings with him, I believed I could trust him," he added.

Around the time they met, Wexner had several concerns that weighed heavily on him. He had lost a substantial portion of his net worth in the 1987 stock market crash and needed help with his investments. He was also building his own town outside Columbus, an ambitious project that let him fulfill his lifelong dream of being an architect but that was being hindered by numerous political and bureaucratic obstacles.

Maybe most important, he was dating a woman—or, rather, letting her escort him when he had to attend public events—who was crazy about him and wanted to get married. The woman, who was from a tiny town in central Ohio, had converted to Judaism and changed her last name to "Cohen" in an effort to appease Wexner's domineering mother. But Wexner was desperate to end the relationship with Ms. Cohen. The fashion mogul had fallen in love with someone else.

Wexner's love interest was a young lawyer named Abigail Koppel, a beautiful Georgia belle who was twenty-five years his junior. One friend of Wexner's described her as the "perfect wife" for him. After decades of loneliness, Wexner had finally met his match in his midfifties. But Koppel also came from a "very traditional, conservative family," according to the friend. Rumors about Wexner's sexuality, which were rampant in Columbus for years, might not sit well.

The billionaire dispatched his new friend Epstein to deliver the breakup news to Ms. Cohen—and, allegedly, a nondisclosure agreement. Bob Fitrakis, a reporter for the *Columbus Free Press*, recalled running into Wexner's old flame at a party after the breakup.

"She told me a story about how she had an agreement, a nondisclosure clause . . . a seven-figure check," said Fitrakis. "Delivered by Epstein with 'Don't ever contact Mr. Wexner again.'"

It was unclear what the purpose of the nondisclosure agreement was, but Fitrakis said the ex-girlfriend claimed at the time that Wexner was bisexual. She was also "very afraid of Jeff Epstein," according to Fitrakis.

"People will not say anything negative [about Wexner]," said Dianne Morosky, the wife of Wexner's longtime vice-chairman at the Limited, Robert Morosky, in an interview. "They'll think it. They'll talk about it to each other, but they won't say it publicly. And they're afraid of him, too, because of his power."

Wexner's problems also seemed to go away after Epstein entered his life and started taking the reins. His financial portfolio recovered. He ended up marrying Koppel. And he moved his new bride into a home in the dream town he was finally able to build—New Albany, Ohio, an ode to his wife's hometown of Albany, Georgia.

Just a couple years before he reportedly met Epstein, Wexner had added to his portfolio with the purchase of a small San Francisco lingerie chain, Victoria's Secret, which he bought for a mere million dollars when it had only six stores. Over the coming decades he'd grow it into the behemoth it is known as today—a thousand stores in 2014 and sales of $7.2 billion.

But Wexner did not excel at managing money, nor did he pay much attention to it. When in the 1980s his company was buying the plus-size brand Lane Bryant, Wexner cared about the idea of the takeover, but not about the share purchase price.

"He didn't understand the numbers," Wexner's former financial adviser Sandy Lewis told *Vanity Fair*.[2] "He's never understood numbers. This is not his strength. This man is a genius at dressing women. This is a guy who feels what they feel. That's his strength. And I figured that out when I first met him and I don't know how he got that set up in his brain but in his soul, he has a sense of how people feel when they wear his clothing. And that's a gift. That's just what it is. Some guys write music, this guy knows how to dress women. He's very, very talented."

As talented as he was, he did not seem to be a particularly good judge of character. At age fifty-four, the cautious Wexner turned over the keys to his multibillion-dollar financial empire to a mystery man from Coney Island whose short career in finance had included a termination from Bear Stearns for financial improprieties and a stint at what was then the largest Ponzi scheme in U.S. history. What nobody in Columbus could figure out was why.

Lewis had thought he would turn on him. He felt blindsided when the would-be clothing mogul turned to Epstein, instead of allowing Lewis to manage and invest his finances.

This upset Lewis, who believed Epstein was a "con artist," he said in his interview with *Vanity Fair*. "I can't imagine, frankly, why a man of his intelligence would simply hand the controls over to another guy," Lewis said, attributing it to Wexner's loneliness.[3] "And this con artist, this fucking idiot, comes into his life . . . My feeling is that he had been seduced. And I don't mean seduced in a physical sense, I mean emotionally seduced out of his loneliness to trust this guy and he figures, he's so fucking smart he can trust anybody."

Perhaps Wexner trusted Epstein with his business because he had helped him with his relationships. Perhaps it was because of tax strategies or other recommendations. Perhaps it was simply because of timing. Or perhaps there was another factor altogether.

Around this time another thing happened that rocked Wexner's financial world. His primary tax lawyer, Arthur Shapiro, was brutally murdered in Columbus in 1985. The still-unsolved murder had ties to the mob, Bob Fitrakis of the *Columbus Free Press* would report. It would rock the small city; Fitrakis would later discover that police started investigating whether Shapiro's work as the Limited's attorney had led to his murder. According to a 1991 memo from the Columbus Police Department's Organized Crime Bureau, Shapiro could have had knowledge of Wexner's bribing public officials in Ohio. The findings "lead to a question of ethics and legality of other unknown transactions and associates with which Wexner may be involved," said the memo. "Arthur Shapiro could have answered too many of these sorts of questions, and might have been forced to answer them in his impending Grand Jury hearing."

According to the memo, Wexner's company had substantial business dealings with the mob, through its connection with Walsh Trucking, a New Jersey trucking company affiliated with the Genovese crime family. The head of Walsh Trucking, Frank Walsh, who was later convicted of racketeering, had even been using the Limited's Columbus office as his mailing address, according to the memo. The connection raised questions in the minds of police when Shapiro, who had insight into Wexner's finances, was killed by the mob. But nothing ever came of the memo, and no one was ever charged with the murder, though there was also a suspect unrelated to Wexner who was later found to have killed another one of his business associates.

Whatever the reason, Shapiro's death left a key position in Wexner's orbit open. He would need someone to help him with taxes.

Epstein professed expertise in this area. He was of course neither a lawyer nor an accountant. Yet his ease with numbers and his dazzling mind would be able to tackle complex ideas, especially transnational tax shelters and tricks.

Steven Hoffenberg, the former chairman of Towers Financial Corporation who himself had his own complex dealings with Epstein, said in an interview, "Epstein bonded with Wexner over a couple of years initially."

In fact, the relations became so close, so quickly that Wexner eventually allowed Epstein to make every financial decision of his life on his behalf. "Eventually, he took over managing my personal finances. He was given power of attorney as is common in that context, and he had wide latitude to act on my behalf with respect to my personal finances while I focused on building my company and undertaking philanthropic efforts," Wexner has said.

Epstein was known to have helped Wexner with the building and decoration of his sixty-thousand-square-foot villa in New Albany, Ohio.

Wexner had undertaken a somewhat bizarre social experiment— buy up tons of land, just outside Columbus, turning it essentially into a company town for executives of his L Brands. It was an enormous undertaking, the purchase, development, and sale of ten thousand acres. The project wasn't going well.

"Before Epstein came along in 1988, the financial preparations and groundwork for the New Albany development were a total mess," Fitrakis told *New York* magazine.[4] "Epstein cleaned everything up, as well as serving Wexner in other capacities—such as facilitating visits to Wexner's home of the crew from *Cats* and organizing a Tony Randall song-and-dance show put on in Columbus."

Epstein in fact at some point purchased his own New Albany home near Wexner's so that they could be even closer. It was the second most valuable home in the area. (He purchased it in 1994 and gave it to Wexner, for free, in 2007.) But he preferred socializing at Wexner's. Eventually, their social circles began to merge.

Epstein's attorney Alan Dershowitz remembers his client inviting him to a dinner at Wexner's.

"It was just men, which I didn't like. I remember calling my wife halfway through, telling her this was boring . . . [Wexner] was married and already had at least one or two kids; they were running around the house, I remember. But his wife was not at the dinner," Dershowitz recalled in an interview.

"The only people at the dinner I remember is Shimon Peres, who talked a lot about art because Wexner has a beautiful art collection including some major Picassos. So Shimon talked a lot about Picasso. And John Glenn, who was then a United States senator from Ohio, was there. The man who at the time owned Sotheby's was there. And Jeffrey was there, and I was there, and Wexner was there," he said.

"But that was a relatively small dinner party and a very serious intellectual discussion. We talked a lot about the Middle East as well because of Shimon Peres being there, and I'm very interested in the Middle East and so is Leslie Wexner. So the two subjects that dominated were the Middle East and art. And then I flew back with [Epstein] that night on his plane, he dropped me off in Boston. And then the next time I saw him was at Harvard."

The Boeing Epstein liked best and possibly used to shuttle Dershowitz to and fro for the party? That, the pilot David Rodgers has said in court documents, was previously owned by Wexner, or one of his many companies. But it was Epstein who dubbed it the Lolita Express.

It would be the same plane Epstein used for his trip to Africa with Bill Clinton, Kevin Spacey, and Chris Tucker. It was, after all, one of the things Clinton found most attractive about his new friend.

To friends, Epstein would either say he ran money for billionaires or, one recalls, simply say he ran only Wexner's money.

A source who would go on to become good friends with Epstein recalls when he first met him asking, "How do you make money?"

"Well, I'm paid to manage every part of Wexner's life," Epstein replied.

"Every part?" the friend asked, fishing for more details.

"Yes," Epstein confirmed. "If he gets up to go to the bathroom, I'm there to help."

In an interview, the friend commented, "And so he was Wexner's boy. And so Wexner is literally who gave him that house in New York."

Which is very likely true. Some press reports suggest Wexner was paid $20 million for the New York mansion, reportedly the largest residence in the city. Real estate records do not reveal a purchase price, because the property was shielded in a trust, so there's no public paper trail to confirm any money was ever paid. The property was officially transferred in December 2011.

"Nobody gives their financial adviser a huge mansion. It's Seventy-first and Fifth. I'm sorry, that just doesn't happen," a former Wall Street executive said in an interview.

Talking more broadly about the Epstein story, a good friend of Epstein's added, "Wexner is the unspoken subplot here."

—

Epstein was probably never a billionaire. Perhaps never even close. But he was nevertheless extremely rich.

The best, most accurate accounting of the financier's finances was what he turned over to the court upon his second and final arrest, less than a month before he would be dead.

His total assets, according to his filing with the court, were listed at $559,120,954. (Later, there were reports indicating perhaps his net worth was $100 million greater than the amount disclosed in federal court.)

The breakdown is as follows:

Cash: $56,547,773

Fixed income: $14,304,679

Equities: $112,679,138

Hedge funds and private equity: $194,986,301

Properties: $180,603,063

9 East Seventy-first Street, Manhattan, New York, estimated to be worth: $55,931,000

49 Zorro Ranch Road, Stanley, New Mexico, estimated to be worth: $17,246,208

358 El Brillo Way, Palm Beach, Florida, estimated to be worth: $12,380,209

22 Avenue Foch, Paris, France, estimated to be worth: $8,672,823

Great St. James Island, Virgin Islands, estimated to be worth: $22,498,600

Little St. James Island, Virgin Islands, estimated to be worth: $63,874,223

The assets are consistent with the amount of money some believe Epstein made from Wexner directly. *The New York Times* has reported that Epstein received assets worth $100 million previously owned by Wexner or his companies: the New York mansion, the New Albany mansion (which was later sold), and the Boeing airplane. That sum does not include payments received by Epstein.

"I've had people say it was a billion dollars, which I discount, or $200 million. I'm thinking more in the $400 or $500 million range," the Columbus-based journalist Bob Fitrakis said in an interview. "And the question is, there's always a question is, how much did Les know he was taking? He had absolute durable power of attorney to get rid of his properties, his assets, move stuff everywhere."

There's also the fact that Wexner has accused Epstein of stealing more than $46 million. The details are hazy. Wexner is an extremely private guy and has taken most opportunities to keep his head down and to not comment on his relationship with Epstein. The eighty-two-year-old these days prefers reclusiveness. He's now married, with four kids.

Yet after Epstein was arrested for the second time, in 2019, but days before his death, Wexner addressed shareholders of his L Brands holding company about his controversial relationship with his ex-consigliere.

"We discovered that he had misappropriated vast sums of money from me and my family," Wexner stated in an August 2019 letter.[5] "This was, frankly, a tremendous shock, even though it clearly pales in comparison to the unthinkable allegations against him now."

The amount of money, financial press reporters would soon say, was in excess of $46 million.

Wexner indicated he was able to get some of the money returned.

But $46 million alone, depending on when it was taken and how it was spent, could account for all of Epstein's assets at the end of his life.

That is, if Epstein had simply invested that sum in an S&P index fund that returned over that period on average roughly 10 percent, compound interest alone, with no further investments, he would have netted more than $800 million. Plus, the properties have appreciated in value quite a bit since Epstein acquired them, and some were allegedly not acquired with money.

Of course a full financial forensic account of Epstein's finances has never been publicly released. (There's no indication one has ever been performed, nor is there any sign that Epstein's remaining trust has ever authorized such an expedition either.)

—

Wexner's money was not the only benefit afforded to Epstein. The financier also took advantage of his client and friend's connections to the modeling industry.

In May 1997, Epstein was in California and met the model Alicia Arden, whom he invited back to his hotel room. She was, Epstein told her at the time, being asked to try out for a spot in the prestigious catalog the company produced.

"She met the suspect, Jeffrey Epstein, at Shutters Hotel for a modeling interview," a police officer would write in a May 20, 1997, Santa Monica Police Department report.[6]

"During the interview Epstein told her to undress and actually assisted her to do so while saying, 'Let me manhandle you for a second,'" the police report added, going on to allege assault.

"Epstein groped her buttocks against her will while acting as though as he was evaluating her body . . . [A]t one point Epstein asked her to undress a second time [and he] actually assisted her by pulling her blouse up and pulling her skirt up and groping her buttocks."

The reason she was there in the first place, despite being hesitant to be so, was the power of the Victoria's Secret catalog. Being featured in the glossy could make a career.

Nevertheless, the accusation, which was first reported by *The New York Times* in 2019, never led to further punishment.

After this alleged assault, Wexner did nothing to distance his consigliere from his personal life or his company.

"Why would someone that powerful and successful befriend someone like Jeffrey Epstein?" Arden told the *Times*, speaking of Wexner.[7] "I don't get it."

It was one of the first warning signs about Epstein that would go unprosecuted by law enforcement. His friends also did not heed the warnings.

An L Brands spokeswoman told the *Times*, "While Mr. Epstein served as Mr. Wexner's personal money manager for a period that ended nearly 12 years ago, we do not believe he was ever employed by nor served as an authorized representative of the company."

The first recorded warning of Epstein's predatory ways received by law enforcement officials would also go unpunished. And it would also, at least tangentially, involve Wexner.

That summer Maria Farmer, Epstein's first known victim, was brought to Ohio to visit Wexner. She was familiar with Wexner before the visit. "Epstein told me what their relationship was. He said Wexner would do anything for him. He bragged about it," she told CBS.

She even says that she referred to Wexner as "The Wizard of Oz" because "he was the one behind the curtain that had all the power."

At the Wexner house, Farmer alleges that Epstein and Maxwell "asked me to come into a bedroom with them and then proceeded to sexually assault me against my will. I fled from the room and called the sheriff's office but did not get any response. The Wexners' security staff refused to let me leave the property. I pleaded with them and my father drove up from Kentucky to Ohio to help me. I was held against my will for approximately 12 hours until I was ultimately allowed to leave with my father."

The Wexners have denied Farmer's claims, telling CBS they "never met her, never spoke with her."[8]

Farmer reported her alleged assault to the Federal Bureau of Investigation, which she says did not pursue an investigation, despite the evidence of her witness testimony.

—

The connection between Epstein and Wexner went deep. When Wexner was building his 316-foot yacht, *Limitless*, Epstein was involved in the minutiae. "He didn't take B.S. from anybody," the ship's ex-captain told *The New York Times* about Epstein.[9] (Epstein, however, did not like boating; he'd "look at a glass of water and get seasick," the ex-captain said.)

More curiously, the two were connected through a series of obscure business ventures and charitable foundations. The complex web will never be unraveled without the help of Epstein, who of course is dead, and Wexner, who remains hidden. But serious accusations of financial shenanigans have been levied, with strong evidence suggesting that the money, for the most part, was not going to charity but straight into Epstein's pocket.

That is, it's likely the charitable trusts have been avenues for Epstein to pay himself off with Wexner's money. Bloomberg's Joe Nocera discovered how this scheme might have worked.[10]

"In a 13D filed in late March 2002, Epstein is listed as trustee or co-trustee for the Wexner Children's Trust II, which held 1.3 percent of L Brands stock, as well as something called Health and Science Interests II, which held 3 percent of the shares. (Wexner himself held 15 percent of the stock.) The document shows that on March 26, Wexner moved 15 million shares, worth over $250 million, from the Wexner Children's Trust, which he solely controlled, to the Health and Science Interests II, where he was a co-trustee with Epstein. The next day, Health and Science Interests II sold 49,800 shares at $17.50 a share," Nocera reported.

"It is possible that the sale was simply a diversification move—though . . . Epstein had never registered with the SEC as an investment professional. It seems more likely that it was a way to put money in Epstein's pocket. There are a half-dozen 13Ds that show a similar pattern: Wexner transfers L Brands stock from trust he solely controls to one where Epstein is a trustee. Within days, the Epstein-managed trust sold the stock."

Reporters for ABC News would go further in tracking the money ties between Wexner and Epstein. "Records show that between 1991 and 2006, Epstein oversaw the sale, mostly through the New York Stock Exchange, of more than $1.3 billion of company stock held by these trusts, representing a vast pool of cash largely controlled by Epstein," ABC would report in January 2020.[11]

"Much of the money was certainly used for charitable purposes, but . . . a potential pattern appears to emerge, one in which Epstein liquidates large amount of stock on behalf of these trusts and then, shortly after, makes large purchases for himself, including homes, planes, even a private island," the report stated.

Again, this financial forensic accounting is nearly impossible without a clear view into Epstein's and even Wexner's accounts. But the financial relationship is extensive—and all one-sided.

—

Being locked up is usually not considered good for business. Especially if you're supposedly running a client-facing money management firm.

Wexner publicly began separating himself from Epstein. "As the allegations against Mr. Epstein in Florida were emerging, he vehemently denied them. But by early fall 2007, it was agreed that he should step back from the management of our personal finances," Wexner wrote in a letter to his family foundation in 2019.

But Epstein was telling a different story to friends, claiming that his first guilty plea in 2008 was of no major concern, according to a friend who discussed the matter with him.

A good friend was worried about Epstein's income stream from Wexner after the arrest, he revealed in an interview. So he picked up the phone and called him, "How are you going to make a living?"

"Oh, come on, you believed that crap?" the friend recalls Epstein saying on the phone.

The friend adds, "So, Wexner always continued to give to him."

—

So what connected them? What was the subplot? Some think it was blackmail. It had been rumored for years that Wexner was gay. In 1985, *New York* magazine published a piece titled "The Bachelor Billionaire: On Pins and Needles with Leslie Wexner."[12]

With a wink and a nod, the magazine labeled the forty-seven-year-old a "confirmed bachelor."

"He doesn't seem to want a child, and, despite what he says about the perfect woman . . . he seems to be waiting to achieve some mystical harmony and balance in himself first," the author would write.

The magazine would go on to quote Wexner as saying, "A lot of people think because I am not married I am asexual or homosexual, but I enjoy a relationship with a woman."

The article's implication was clear—that the fashionista with an expertise in women's lingerie may not have the hands-on experience someone in his position in the 1980s might have been expected to have. That is, that he may be unfamiliar with the sexual needs of women.

"We all suspected/knew that Les Wexner was gay," says a former Wall Street source whose firm worked with Wexner's. "I've heard that he and Epstein had an affair," the source added. "This is all about keeping that quiet."

Some might laugh at the idea of Epstein's having an affair with Wexner, but these are not the only allegations that he was interested in men—or perhaps boys.

His former friend and colleague Steven Hoffenberg said that Epstein was in fact gay. "He lived in the Solow building on Second Avenue," Hoffenberg explained. He then claimed he never set foot in Epstein's Manhattan apartment because "I didn't want to be in that box. I'm straight. Epstein was not."

Hoffenberg declined to provide further details except to say, "I spent years with him and his activities."

Lynn Forester de Rothschild, the socialite who introduced Epstein to her many friends, including President Bill Clinton, once remarked to a mutual acquaintance that she believed Epstein was gay because he never made a move on her.

Another acquaintance of his remarked, "We always thought he

was gay . . . I thought he was obnoxious, and I thought he hated women. He never seemed affectionate to the women."

Others sources were a bit more circumspect. "I think he was ashamed of being gay, and he was supermacho as the result of it and would have sex with women, would brag about his women," one associate of Epstein's confided. "My own theory was that because he was embarrassed and ashamed and he didn't want anybody to know that he liked boys, but that's speculation."

If Wexner was gay, he could not allow the public to know. "It wouldn't do for a CEO of a big company like the Limited to be gay," the source added. "It was a time when you couldn't do that."

Which best explains the financial concessions that Wexner for years made to Epstein. It was never a fiduciary-client relationship. It was one made up of blackmail and extortion.

And it didn't stop there. It went way beyond just Wexner, especially as Epstein's cachet in America began to wane after he was locked up late in the first decade of the twenty-first century.

"He was blackmailing, you know, shahs and sultans and everything from the Mideast. I think it was blackmailing everybody," said a source.

"That was his business play—blackmail. Not financial services advice," he added. "Please, that's ridiculous."

—

It turns out that in 1996 Bob Fitrakis of the *Columbus Free Press* dug into this story. He was looking into a local political controversy when he first came across the name Jeffrey Epstein.

Southern Air Transport, then a scandal-plagued, CIA-owned airline that gained infamy in the 1980s for shuttling weapons to the contras and trafficking cocaine, had abruptly decided to move its world headquarters to Columbus, Ohio. The city's wealthiest man, Leslie Wexner, was rumored to be behind the move and was using the planes to transport merchandise to his Limited stores.

"We were looking at a story on how Southern Air Transport came to Columbus. How did this CIA-connected airline end up in Columbus? And people said, well, it's Wexner. But it's not really Wexner. Epstein's handling all the logistics for him," said Fitrakis.

Fitrakis started asking around about Epstein, a supposed money manager from Manhattan whom local officials would jokingly refer to as "Les's gal Friday." Wexner's relationship with Epstein had seemed to materialize out of nowhere and was a puzzle to many in Columbus. The L Brands founder was a deliberate and deeply shy man, born and raised in Ohio, who dressed in carefully coordinated suits and didn't marry until he was middle-aged. Epstein, with his booming Brooklyn accent, tracksuits, and unabashed social climbing, was a different breed.

Fitrakis soon learned that Epstein had consolidated enormous power over Wexner's life and finances in just a few years after the two met in the mid-1980s. The Limited founder had gifted Epstein a $70 million home in Manhattan, put him at the helm of his family's foundations, and signed over durable power of attorney—allowing Epstein unrestricted access to Wexner's billions.

When Fitrakis checked with his sources from the Ohio inspector general's office, he found that Epstein was also on their radar.

"They used to call [Epstein] 'the boyfriend,'" said Fitrakis. "There was concern by the inspector general; they were concerned whether or not Epstein was blackmailing Wexner."

"Everyone thought [Wexner] was enthralled. I mean, they thought it was like Rasputin," he said. "And a lot of them suspected it was sexual."

14

The Smart Set

Brockman, Dershowitz, and the "Intellectual Enablers"

What does that got to do with pussy!
JEFFREY EPSTEIN

R eal money managers are single-minded. Their days and nights revolve around markets, currencies, and anything else that might further their—and their clients'—financial interests. That was not Jeffrey Epstein.

Instead, he spent hours every day preying on underage girls and actively sought to cultivate an aura of intellectualism. He liked to think of himself as a man of many sophisticated interests, perhaps to mask his baser activities.

Epstein's "best pal for decades" was the artist and scientist Stuart Pivar, who is now ninety years old. They became close as fellow board members of the New York Academy of Art, which Pivar founded with Andy Warhol. "I adored him," Pivar told *Mother Jones* in an interview.[1]

They also had business dealings together. Pivar would act as a kind of consultant for Epstein, offering advice on what sorts of artworks he should purchase and how he might decorate his many homes. Pivar claims, however, that Epstein routinely ignored his advice and took active pleasure in buying fakes. "He was amused to put one over on the world by having fake art," his friend now recalls.

But Pivar liked him and credits his friend with doing "amazing, incredible, amazing, remarkable things for science" by uniting intellectuals and funding, or mostly promising to fund, many of their ventures. "He brought together scientists for the sake of trying to inculcate some kind of a higher level of scientific thought, even though he himself didn't know shit from Shinola about science," Pivar told the magazine. "He never knew nothing about anything."

Epstein did not let his limited knowledge, nor lack of education, get in the way of gathering some of the smartest minds—on a regular basis. "In his peculiarly inquiring mind, let's say, like a child who is fresh to the world—because he has no compunction about approaching people—he brought together the most important scientists like Stephen Gould, like Pinker, like all of those people, and myself even, at dinners, and would propose interesting, naive ideas. Steve Pinker describes that," Pivar recalled.

He would often interrupt these high-level gatherings with some of the strangest—simplest—questions. "Oh, what is gravity?" Epstein would ask, for example. His dinner guests would be flummoxed. "And because he was Jeffrey, why, they would—and as the founder of the feast—they would listen to him and try to give [answers]. He was attempting, somehow, in his ignorant and scientifically naive state, to do something scientifically important," Pivar recalled.

Perhaps Epstein was amusing himself by mocking academics—just as he mocked the art world by hanging up frauds around his house.

But why were some of the academically praised minds so keen to gather with Epstein, only to be bombarded with questions asking to define gravity? Why were they so willing to sign up to be mocked, and what did the smart set see in this unconversant college dropout that kept them coming back for more? Simple: money. "He had no compunctions about inviting people, and since he had money, they would listen. He would promise money to people and, of course, never come across, by the way. That's what's called a dangler. Didn't he promise $15 million to Harvard? I don't know if they got two cents," Pivar said.

In fact, Harvard received more than two cents from Epstein. Between 1998 and 2007, it received at least $8.9 million from the child predator, the university's president, Lawrence Bacow, admitted in a 2019 statement. A 2003 gift of $6.5 million went to the Program for Evolutionary Dynamics, while $2.4 million went elsewhere. Bacow also admitted the university had repaid Epstein's generosity with an honorific designation as a visiting fellow. "Stephen Kosslyn, a former faculty member and a beneficiary of Epstein's philanthropy, designated Epstein as a Visiting Fellow in the Department of Psychology in 2005," Bacow said.

But Pivar is right: Epstein had promised much more philanthropy to the institution. Rarely did his promises match reality.

Epstein had pledged a total of $30 million to the Program for Evolutionary Dynamics, which came about when Professor Martin Nowak, a biologist and mathematician, visited Epstein's private island.

"Jeffrey was the perfect host," Nowak noted in his book *SuperCooperators: Altruism, Evolution, and Why We Need Each Other to*

Succeed, published in 2011. "I asked a casual question about what it was like to dive in the warm, clear waters around the island. The very next day a scuba diving instructor turned up. When the British cosmologist Stephen Hawking came to visit, and remarked that he had never been underwater, Jeffrey rented a submarine for him."

The rest of the money never came through. Despite apparently coming up $23.5 million short of his stated pledge to Harvard's Program for Evolutionary Dynamics, Epstein would continue to state falsely that he had given the money.

And when Epstein faced legal problems after the Palm Beach police began looking into his sexual crimes in 2005, Harvard took a principled stand—to keep every last dollar Epstein had given it. "Mr. Epstein's gift is funding important research using mathematics to study areas such as evolutionary theory, viruses, and cancers," Harvard said through a spokesman to the school newspaper on September 12, 2006. "The University is not considering returning this gift."

But at least for Harvard, there does appear to have been a distancing; Bacow now says that the university didn't accept money from Epstein after his guilty plea. (There's still evidence that he maintained a relationship with Nowak as late as 2014, however.)

Which for Epstein was no problem. He found a more welcoming environment just down the street in Cambridge at the Massachusetts Institute of Technology. An MIT investigation, conducted by lawyers retained by the university to investigate its ties to Epstein and released in 2020, discovered that before his legal problems the institution of higher education accepted one donation of $100,000. But after his 2008 guilty plea, MIT accepted $750,000 distributed in nine donations.

"The post-conviction donations," the lawyers' report disclosed,[2] "were all made either to support the work of the Media Lab ($525,000) or Professor of Mechanical Engineering and Engineering Systems and Physics Seth Lloyd ($225,000)." An additional sum of money, $60,000, was totally off the books—given from Epstein directly to Professor Lloyd's personal bank account.

Most damning for MIT was that "members of the Senior Team who approved MIT's acceptance of Epstein's donations were aware that Epstein had a criminal record involving sex offenses." And with that money, Epstein became somewhat of a fixture around campus— visiting at least nine times between 2013 and 2017.

In the report, which was released after Epstein's 2019 death, MIT lawyers concluded that Epstein was attempting to "launder his reputation by associating himself with reputable individuals and institutions."

Which at least is partly true. By being seen with professors and by being tied to prestigious universities, Epstein hoped to be seen as an intellectual himself.

But perhaps the most explosive allegations in the report would be that Epstein had secured donations from his wealthy friends for MIT. "In 2014, Epstein claimed to have arranged for Microsoft cofounder Bill Gates to provide an anonymous $2 million donation to the Media Lab. He also claimed that same year to have arranged for a $5 million anonymous donation to the Media Lab from Leon Black, the co-founder of Apollo Global Management," the report stated.

These allegations were surprising for no other reason than that they signified a closeness between Epstein and Gates, and between Epstein and Leon Black, that both powerful and rich men had strenuously sought to avoid. (Gates, for his part, denied to MIT that Epstein had anything to do with his financial support for the university.)

"Gates and the $51 billion Gates Foundation have championed the well-being of young girls," *The New York Times* would note.[3] "By the time Gates and Epstein first met, Epstein had served jail time for soliciting prostitution from a minor and was required to register as a sex offender."

That first meeting was in 2011, well after he had been publicly shamed by his guilty plea. The relationship would continue, with Gates playing down how close the pair was or denying that there was ever a direct financial relationship.

"His lifestyle is very different and kind of intriguing although it would not work for me," the Microsoft mogul would tell colleagues in an email in 2011. The pair apparently mulled the idea of a philanthropic partnership, though there's no proof that they ever went forward with it.

—

The MIT report also suggested that central to Epstein's efforts at MIT was John Brockman, the prominent New York literary agent. He had been the one to make some of these connections with professors.

The writer Evgeny Morozov, a client of Brockman's, has dubbed his agent "Jeffrey Epstein's Intellectual Enabler"[4] for allegedly opening his Rolodex to the child predator. The head of the MIT Media Lab, who accepted most of the money from Epstein received by the university, Joi Ito, was a client of Brockman's. Same with Steven Pinker, Daniel Dennett, Marvin Minsky, and a slew of other leading thinkers on science and technology who would over the years socialize directly with Brockman, of course, and his buddy Epstein.

Brockman tried to get Morozov to mingle with Epstein too. "Jeffrey

Epstein, the billionaire science philanthropist, showed up at this week-end's event by helicopter (with his beautiful young assistant from Belarus). He'll be in Cambridge in a couple of weeks [and] asked me who he should meet. You are one of the people I suggested and I told him I would send some links," the agent wrote to his client.

"He's the guy who gave Harvard #30m [*sic*] to set up Martin Nowak. He's been extremely generous in funding projects of many of our friends and clients. He also got into trouble and spent a year in jail in Florida," he explained. "If he contacts you it's probably worth your time to meet him as he's extremely bright and interesting."

Morozov correctly concludes that Brockman wasn't just network-ing. He was, instead, "acting as Epstein's PR man—his liaison with the world of scientists and intellectuals that Brockman had cultivated."

For many intellectuals, getting paid a professor's salary, working with Brockman represented the real chance that they'd receive hand-some checks from prestigious popular publishers. Sure, most had been successful before, but only in academic settings, earning academic royalties for routinely ignored work. Being a client of Brockman's would change that. All of a sudden a two-page book proposal could generate an advance worth hundreds of thousands of dollars and a contract with a publisher with widespread distribution. For many wealthy people, association with Brockman meant entrée into a world of supreme thinkers that might otherwise be confined to the academy.

"In Brockman's world, billionaires, scientists, artists, novelists, journalists, and musicians all blend together to produce enormous value—for each other and, of course, for Brockman," Morozov ob-served. Everyone benefited. The insecure wealthy elite got to rub shoulders with leading academics, while the leading academics got to be fawned over and directly pitch their research projects to men who could single-handedly fund their most ambitious work.

Brockman's organizing vehicle for his commingling of business was the Edge Foundation, which hosted dinners and get-togethers for many of his clients and friends. It was funded in large part by Epstein, who gave the nonprofit charity $638,000 between 2001 and 2015 and was at times the foundation's only financial supporter.

—

The most successful in America do not need the trappings of a business suit and tie. Think Steve Jobs (in his black turtlenecks), Mark Zuckerberg (known to don hoodies), and Bill Gates (usually gracing charitable events in a pair of khakis). These titans of industry are so famous, so rich, so successful that they can wear whatever the hell they want.

It's a demonstration of what the economist Tyler Cowen calls "countersignaling," which he explains "is when you go out of your way to show you don't need to go out of your way."[5]

At America's fanciest restaurants, for instance, the richest and most famous are not the ones wearing jackets. They wear jeans with holes, T-shirts, and—gasp!—flip-flops.

Which explains the Jeffrey Epstein ethos. Yes, he was a college dropout from a decidedly lower-middle-class upbringing. But that's not the image he sought to project to his friends and patrons.

Instead, he hated dressing up, shunning fancy clothes for casual college sweatshirts, jeans, fancy slippers. He wanted everyone around to know just how important he was, by being the least dressed-up person in the room.

Epstein's favorite hoodie, perhaps, showed off whom he wanted to be associated with. It was a crimson Harvard quarter zip with a kangaroo pocket and a drawstring hood. He loved it. Not just because of the obvious cozy comfort it provided, but because it showed off what an intellectual he wanted everyone to believe he was.

There are few who knew him who dispute that. He had gifts. Mathematics, piano playing, and cunning charm.

The intellectuals—that is, the academic elite—were also curious about him. Throughout his life, but especially after he accumulated wealth, Epstein cultivated deep and financial relationships with the foremost minds in America.

"Jeffrey had lots and lots and lots of dough. Scientists are always looking for lots and lots of dough, because most scientists spend most of their time writing grant proposals to raise money. Jeffrey didn't require a grant proposal. Jeffrey would promise money and so they crowded around, and he also was an extremely personable, amusing kind of person to talk to. He was full of incredible ideas. He was charming in the extreme, and that's why everyone paid attention to him," Stuart Pivar explained in his interview with *Mother Jones*.[6]

To many who spent time with him, the former Dalton teacher's interest in ideas seemed real. Alan Dershowitz recalls many times, myriad meetings and dinners, that centered on sharing and exploring ideas.

—

In the late 1990s, Dershowitz was vacationing in Martha's Vineyard when he got an unexpected phone call from Lord Rothschild's then fiancée, Lynn Forester.

Forester—described by one friend as Epstein's "social pimp" before she had a falling-out with the financier over a real estate deal—launched into a high-pressure sales pitch.

"My good friend Jeffrey Epstein is coming to town," she said. "Do you know who he is?"

Dershowitz had no idea.

"He'd like to come over and meet you; he's heard very good things about you, that you're a smart guy," said Forester.

Dershowitz wasn't interested. He had been planning to spend time at home with his kids. But Forester was persistent. "Alan, please, just do me a big favor," she said. "Just let him drop by for an hour, talk, meet him." Finally, the Harvard law professor relented.

Epstein knew how to flatter his hosts. Although he never drank alcohol, he showed up at Dershowitz's house with a bottle of Dom Pérignon champagne tucked under his arm.

"He met my kids, my wife. Then we went out on my deck and we talked for a little bit, all about academics, about how he was setting up a process of evolutionary psychology," said Dershowitz in an interview. Before long, Epstein had invited him to fly on his private jet to a birthday party he was throwing for billionaire Leslie Wexner. Epstein claimed that Wexner had asked him to bring the "smartest man" he had met that year, and that just so happened to be Dershowitz.

"He wanted to get to know me," Dershowitz explained. And he wanted to know Dershowitz's friends. "He wanted me to introduce him to some of my colleagues, which I did. And he introduced me to people, like George Church, the man who decoded the genome, who was on our faculty [at Harvard] but I'd never met him. And then [Epstein] would have these seminars at Harvard. He rented an office, and about once every month or so he would have one of these seminars where fantastic people would come from MIT, people he knew, the leading lights: Noam Chomsky; Marvin Minsky, the developer of artificial intelligence; George Church; David Gergen . . . Steven Pinker. All the leading lights were there," he said.

"It was an honor to be invited. I went and I enjoyed these events thoroughly; we did have boxed lunches sometimes, and we'd sit around for one and a half, two hours and discuss biology. And he would be kind of like the master of ceremonies, raising hard questions. Or sometimes somebody would present a paper, and we would critique the paper. But it was purely, purely academic. And there were never any young people around. I can't imagine any of the people who were there would have stayed if they saw anything inappropriate."

—

If academics had not had their heads in the sand, perhaps they too would have seen the warning signs. Because Epstein was prone to outbursts. Unusual, shocking, and vulgar displays in front of his scholarly crowd, according to one member.

"So people would come to his dinners, including myself. I even had them," Pivar recalls. "Jeffrey brought these people together and thought that he was causing basic thought processes to happen, which he sort of was, even though they were sort of irrelevant. I mean, to bring together a bunch of scientists and say, what is gravity? Which is ridiculous in a way, even though it's a question nobody can answer. But he would do that kind of stuff. Just for the sake of, I don't know what. And Jaron Lanier and all that group, the greatest thinkers that they were, he brought together with a purpose of thinking, rightfully or wrongfully, that he was going to introduce some kind of logic or something—some special kind of a thought process, which others hadn't thought of, which of course is absurd.

"While everybody was watching, we began to realize he didn't know what he was talking about. Then after a couple of minutes—Jeffrey had no attention span whatsoever—he would interrupt the conversation and change it and say things like 'What does that got to do with pussy!'" Pivar remembered.

Moreover, when he did express ideas—and not just shout "pussy"—he offered some of the most radical views one can imagine. He argued in favor of eugenics, masked by a stringent view of science.

For Epstein, the biological sciences were particularly intriguing. "He thought everything was biological. He was very focused on biology," said Dershowitz.

"He was not religious," Dershowitz said in an interview. "He was fascinated by the law and science."

Epstein in time would become an advocate of transhumanism. *The New York Times*, which first reported Epstein's view on this matter, defined the ideology as "the science of improving the human population through technologies like genetic engineering and artificial intelligence."[7]

"On multiple occasions starting in the early 2000s, Mr. Epstein told scientists and businessmen about his ambitions to use his New Mexico ranch as a base where women would be inseminated with his sperm and would give birth to his babies, according to two award-winning scientists and an adviser to large companies and wealthy individuals, all of whom Mr. Epstein told about it," the *Times* reported in 2019, a week and a half before he died in a Manhattan holding cell.

"Once, at a dinner at Mr. Epstein's mansion on Manhattan's Upper

East Side, [the author Jaron] Lanier said he talked to a scientist who told him that Mr. Epstein's goal was to have 20 women at a time impregnated at his 33,000-square-foot Zorro Ranch in a tiny town outside Santa Fe."

At another event, Epstein praised cryonics, stating he "wanted his head and penis to be frozen."

He also donated $20,000 to the World Transhumanist Association, whose stated mission is "to deeply influence a new generation of thinkers who dare to envision humanity's next steps," and personally financed individual transhumanist advocates.

Dershowitz, and other academics, now claim to have pushed back against these radical views.

Nevertheless, Epstein maintained a collection of impressive friends: the evolutionary biologist Stephen Jay Gould, the cognitive psychologist Steven Pinker, and the molecular biologist Richard Axel, among others.

"I met Jeffrey Epstein at discussions at a research center at Harvard," explained Noam Chomsky in an email exchange. "Neither I, nor as far as I know any others, had a sense that he was trying to ingratiate himself or anything else . . . He was participating, and sometimes brought with him some outstanding mathematicians and scientists, who we were all pleased to have join the discussions."

There was another reason so many scientists were interested in Epstein, but few would acknowledge it publicly.

"For money, you understand, this was going on, why he had all these scientist friends," said one academic who was close with the financier. "He had a lot of money, he was known to give it away, so a zillion people would show up asking for it.

"The feeling of pretension was important to him," he added. "I didn't get it. But he was always visiting another academic for no reason."

Keeping an academically impressive crew around him nearly always left Epstein the richest man in the room. And, therefore, in certain ways the most powerful. Money, even (and perhaps especially) among academics, is an alluring elixir.

—

But for some, keeping Epstein around might have been out of sympathy. Pivar believes his buddy was "totally, totally, totally, totally misunderstood."

While he claims to have cut ties with Epstein after Maria Farmer, one of the first known accusers of sexual misconduct, confided in him that she had been held against her will by Epstein and his buddy Ghislaine Maxwell, he believes Epstein acted out because of a medical condition.

"The peculiar thing is, let's put it this way, now that you've got me thinking: Jeffrey had a severe case of what's called satyriasis, the male counterpart of nymphomania. Except that he had the money and the wherewithal to work it out, to manage to supply himself with three underage girls every single day," Pivar told *Mother Jones*.[8]

"Who knows how many men have that? And the difference is that if there are other ones who have it, I don't know, they probably go around raping or God knows what they do. Jeffrey had the money to do it politely—namely, by getting [complacent] young girls."

So for some in the smart set, Epstein was a psychological tragedy, not a psycho sex fiend. "If Jeffrey Epstein was found guilty of fooling around with one 16-year-old trollop, nobody would pay any attention," Pivar asserted, bizarrely framing it as a "quantitative" problem rather than a "qualitative" one.

▬

Perhaps another reason he developed an interest in a decidedly intellectual cause was to cultivate relationships with charitable enterprises to mask some of his financial shenanigans.

Epstein's donations, on the rare occasions he actually came through with them, were given from his various charitable foundations. He had at least half a dozen, with links to several more. And yet the money that flowed through those foundations appears not to have originated from his own accounts.

Instead, Epstein used the charitable accounts to receive funds from others in his orbit. For instance, his C.O.U.Q. Foundation received a gigantic donation of around $21 million from Leslie Wexner. While his Gratitude America foundation received a hefty donation of $10 million from the investor Leon Black.[9]

The money from Black came in 2015, well after the world was aware of Epstein's admitted sexual crimes. Black also named Epstein a member of the board of his own charitable foundation, but removed him in 2012. (Black claims he was actually removed in 2007 but a clerical error kept him affiliated with his charity for an additional half a decade.)

Black has avoided answering questions about his ties to Epstein, though in a 2019 statement he told his firm, "I was completely unaware of, and am deeply troubled by, the conduct that is now the subject of the federal criminal charges brought against Mr. Epstein."

Whether money received by Epstein's charitable organizations ever made its way directly back to his own personal bank accounts is a matter of wide speculation.

Even so, the tax expert Martin Sheil told *The New York Times* the foundations appeared to him to be acting as Epstein's "piggy banks."[10]

"It doesn't pass the smell test," Sheil told the newspaper.

—

Another thing happened in 2015 to once again thrust Epstein in the news: the gossip site *Gawker* published "the Holy Grail," the full but redacted contents of the little black book.[11] It was Epstein's full phone book, detailing the contact information for his friends and associates.

"An annotated copy of the address book, which also contains entries for Alec Baldwin, Ralph Fiennes, Griffin Dunne, *New York Post* gossip columnist Richard Johnson, Ted Kennedy, David Koch, filmmaker Andrew Jarecki, and all manner of other people you might expect a billionaire to know, turned up in court proceedings after Epstein's former house manager Alfredo Rodriguez tried to sell it in 2009," the reporter Nick Bryant noted in his *Gawker* piece. "About 50 of the entries, including those of many of Epstein's suspected victims and accomplices as well as [Donald] Trump, [Courtney] Love, [Ehud] Barak, [Alan] Dershowitz, and others, were circled by Rodriguez."

The names were shocking. Many had claimed not to have known Epstein, while even more were never asked. The book proved an intimate connection between those in the phone book and the then admitted sexual predator. As *New York* magazine wrote, the book showed Epstein "deeply enmeshed in the highest social circles."[12]

Epstein's house manager Alfredo Rodriguez had been trying to shop around the book: asking price $50,000. He had unsuccessfully been seeking a payday since 2009.

Indeed, his attempt to sell the information backfired; the FBI got wind of his effort to sell evidence behind their backs, resulting in a stiff eighteen-month sentence. In December 2014, Rodriguez died, allegedly of mesothelioma.[13] Within a month the black book, which had been Rodriguez's "insurance policy" while he was alive, was published.

Ultimately, however, the press did not use the publication of the black book, and the subsequent publication of the private flight logs from Epstein's private jets, as a blueprint to blow the whole sordid story into the open. "Gawker got a lot of hits. They published his flight manifest too. But ultimately I was stunned that no one in the mainstream media was willing to touch the subject matter," the reporter Nick Bryant, who had the amazing scoop, said in 2019.[14]

It'd take more time for more of the story to trickle out.

15
The Media
How Epstein Played the Press

Those who have the gold, rule.

PEGGY SIEGAL

For years Jeffrey Epstein was welcomed and heralded by the media. He was mythologized from the moment he came across their radar, turning this Brooklyn-born nobody into a patron of the poor who traveled on his own dime to Africa to fight one of society's biggest scourges—HIV/AIDS. Media even spent years misreporting the very size of Epstein's wealth, reporting that he was a billionaire, despite there never being a single shred of evidence to confirm his achievement of this feat.

The relationship created problems—for the media. Could we ever trust the people who kept up fawning coverage of this monster for years to tell us what "really happened" in the last moments of his life?

Candace Bushnell, the *Sex and the City* writer who would famously be played by Sarah Jessica Parker in the television series of the same name, began investigating Epstein rumors in 1994. The subject was just her forte; she was after all a sex columnist for *The New York Observer*.

"There was a rogues' gallery of men who there were shady rumors [about], and he was one of those guys," Bushnell recalled in a 2019 interview with *The Hollywood Reporter* shortly before Epstein died.[1]

So Bushnell put on her high heels to do a little shoe leather reporting. "I went to his apartment when a mutual friend got me invited to a cocktail party at his house," she recalls, claiming the town house was "bland" and "hotel-ish."

It wasn't as if she walked into the "models" and "parties on the plane" scenes she had been hearing about. The scene was boring.

So she started asking those milling around about "all kinds of rumors" she had heard. She wanted to know where the private plane was kept and how he got his money. "I was getting information, and then the door flies in and a bodyguard-type [person] walks in asking why I want to know about the plane," she recalled.

And that's about the time her visit to Epstein's ended. She left. The next day she received a call. "This is his lawyer, there's nothing to investigate. Don't investigate him. Don't look into his activities. Don't go up to him at parties. Don't ask questions about him," the person on the phone told Bushnell.

The intimidation and threats worked, Bushnell admits. "You know, I'd like to live," she said.

"It takes a particular kind of reporter to do that kind of story, and it's just not me," she would recall years later.

The sex columnist would not be the only person he would try to intimidate.

—

The strange thing about Jeffrey Epstein's sex trafficking of minors, countless sexual assaults, and alleged rapes is that it's easy to see how, of all things, the election of Donald Trump as president of the United States led to his arrest. And that's not because Trump did anything at all to stop his former friend.

On the contrary, he along with every other famous person in Epstein's orbit (Bill Clinton, Prince Andrew, Leslie Wexner, money managers, media titans) either accepted the wealthy predator as one of their own or quietly rejected him.

Many witnessed Epstein's crimes; some even participated in them. But until his first guilty plea in Florida in 2008, Epstein operated with impunity. Even then, he received an extremely light punishment.

After he served his time, so to speak, Epstein seems to have picked up where he left off. Prosecutors in the U.S. Virgin Islands found evidence that suggests he continued trafficking women and assaulting underage girls, using his financial means and political power to continue the very activities that got him in trouble in the first place.

And yet, no further criminal proceedings followed him for more than a decade, even though he was a known predator of crimes that have extremely high rates of recidivism.

Between arrests, perhaps the only thing that did change was that Epstein finally understood that operating so openly and with such a great media profile could be harmful. So he assumed at least a slightly lower profile than he had before. Gatherings at his home with journalists and newsreaders were more hush-hush. His political donations, which under law would have to be publicly disclosed, were no longer welcome.

But those slight tweaks were reflective of a singular fact: everyone knew that Jeffrey Epstein was a sexual predator whose victims were children. His sweetheart plea deal was known. His association with politicians, academics, and elites was known.

Yet had Hillary Clinton won the 2016 election, one can easily imagine Epstein never facing the renewed scrutiny he began to receive in 2018 when the *Miami Herald* began running its "Perversion of Justice" series. Because the whole reason for that series—or at least one of the rationales for running it—was that the man who cut the sweetheart deal for the feds, the prosecutor Alex Acosta, had been made labor secretary by Trump.

With the election of Trump, many reporters rediscovered a sense of weight and urgency, a new sense of holding the powerful accountable. That's a trait they should always possess, of course. But it seems to be forgotten when liberals are sworn into power, only to be rediscovered four or eight years later.

It is remarkable that it is true both that so much is known about Epstein because of the media and that he was able to operate for so many years because of the media.

He first played the media, using the power of the press to inflate his image (a billionaire, a generous philanthropist, a money manager). And then he hid from it, which was easy enough because no one was looking for him.

Playing the media was an old game for Epstein. In the 1980s, when he began to make waves, New York journalist Jesse Kornbluth became friendly with him and considered writing a book about him.

The moneyman apparently appreciated the attention from Kornbluth. But one episode in 1987 left the writer with nothing but contempt for him.

"My wife-to-be was then a military historian, with a book about to be published. *Interview Magazine* photographed her in a buttoned-up military shirt, with a taut khaki tie. A witty photo of an attractive woman. But not a sexy look. Jeffrey Epstein had chatted her up at a few parties. The military look fooled him not at all," Kornbluth recalled in a reflection upon Epstein's 2019 arrest in an article in *Salon*.[2]

The eve of their wedding, Epstein called up Kornbluth's fiancée. "It's your last free night," Epstein said on the phone. "Why don't you come over and fuck me?"

"That was how . . . Epstein became dead to me," Kornbluth wrote.

Nevertheless, Epstein was not really dead to Kornbluth—or to many other journalists.

Peggy Siegal, a well-connected, hard-charging PR guru, traded favors with Epstein over the years and consequently found herself in the middle of the media storm when her acquaintance would finally face the music in 2019. (In a terse email exchange, she insisted that she had never been on payroll. "Epstein was never my client," she wrote.) Her tale is a cautionary one—a reminder that professionals are often judged by their clients, even if money is never exchanged for their services.

Siegal's bustling business would quickly go kaput, leaving her to lay off eight employees and lose nearly every single one of her paying customers, clients like Netflix, Annapurna Pictures, and FX.

The Peggy Siegal Company had specialized in attracting high-social-net-worth individuals to be interested in films. It had helped pioneer the budding field of Oscar campaigning, a specialized Hollywood field to influence members of the Academy of Motion Picture Arts and Sciences to vote her clients for the most prestigious award in the business. She had poured her life into building up from nothing, but in 2020 it was barely hanging on by a thread.

In a profile in *Vanity Fair*, which she appears to have agreed to as a last-ditch attempt to pour a bucket of water on her burning reputation, Siegal claimed to have no knowledge of Epstein's crimes. "I had no idea about the underage girls," she told the glossy, pleading ignorance to knowing why precisely he faced criminal charges in Florida in 2008.[3]

But then, apparently suddenly, she remembered gently admonishing him. "I'm sure I had said something like, 'You better change your ways,'" Siegal told the magazine. "I mean, I knew him, but I didn't know much about him. Yeah, I spoke to him on the phone. He came to some screenings. I was never privy to his private life. I knew nothing about the girls. Nothing at all."

Which seems particularly strange when one considers that Siegal, who to this day claims that Epstein was no client of hers, arranged the infamous 2010 dinner at Epstein's home with the star guest Prince Andrew that featured the media stars George Stephanopoulos, Katie Couric, Woody Allen, and Chelsea Handler.

The *New York Post* would cover that visit from Prince Andrew on the front page—under the in-your-face-headline "PRINCE & PERV," with the perhaps less subtle subhead "1st Photos: Randy Andy with NYC Sex Creep."[4]

Siegal now claims, "It's so much easier in hindsight, 10 years later, to digest all this information and say, 'Well, of course they knew that' . . . The times have changed so much, in the past five years, that [which] was normal bad behavior between genders is completely out of the realm of possibility today."[5]

But perhaps the most revealing moment in the interview is when Siegal asks the *Vanity Fair* writer, "You know about the golden rule?"

"Do unto others?" the writer suggests.

"No. Those who have the gold, rule," Siegal explains.

—

Reporting the story of Jeffrey Epstein is difficult. He was for years a powerful, rich, and politically connected man who was not afraid to do whatever necessary to get his way. Many in his orbit share those traits.

Even now, a call to his former friends and associates rarely receives even an acknowledgment of receipt. Those who know don't want to say. Those who socialized with him, partied with him, and were perhaps even aware of his most evil vices have no incentive to discuss it.

As one reporter who has extensively covered Epstein sarcastically put it, joking how elites who have refused to speak until now might receive a call, "Yeah, thanks for calling. I'm really glad. I've been waiting to tell everybody about this. And now's my chance. I was afraid that it was going to go away with Epstein's death. But now that you came along, now I can tell you."

Asked what threats he's faced while reporting about Epstein, the reporter in an interview retells his struggle to report on basic information, with firsthand sourcing, because of publishers' fear of aggressive lawyers.

"I had spoken to a billionaire's pilot who was on the record," the reporter said in an interview, "and who was an occasional substitute pilot for Epstein's plane. So he saw a lot of things . . . And even having something on the record was not good enough.

"The letters would come—threatening letters," the reporter said. At which point the publication he worked for would cave. "Hey, you can write things that are less controversial, but you can't write what's really going on," he said, apparently mimicking his editor. "Magazines or newspapers, they just fold the tent as soon as the nasty letter comes from the lawyers. That's the MO nowadays."

The reporter also outlined how the PR professionals who are supposed to help facilitate contact with their wealthy clients and the press are, in fact, really just operating as the first line of offense for lawyers. After a conversation with the PR team, the letters begin to flow from legal, using the language from the media request. "They're just a conduit to the lawyer," he explained.

To say this is unusual is an understatement. It is not normal for reporters to receive legal threats at all. And it's downright rare to receive ones before publication—based on interview requests alone.

"He's dead. But the people you're writing about who interacted with him are very much alive and very rich and very lawyered up. They're like on high alert for this," the reporter added.

Calling one billionaire "evil incarnate" and "ready to strike back," the reporter recalled his run-in and his publication's decision to back down in the face of threats. "One great story I had that they wouldn't let me run was Epstein and Ghislaine having sex in the back of a [billionaire's] plane with [him] sitting there in the passengers' section." But the billionaire's lawyers intervened aggressively with his publisher and killed the story. "They don't want to have anything, you know, even remotely associated with [Epstein]."

Speaking more broadly about the entire media industry caving to the demands of lawyers, the journalist observed, "I think the whole industry's become, post-*Gawker*, much more risk averse and they don't have the financials to back it up anymore. You know, the financial performance. So they're all like hanging by a thread, the last thing they need is to spend $2 million defending a lawsuit against a billionaire."

Which is why reporting on this subject is so difficult and why the Epstein story is as much a media story as it is one about politics, power, and money. For years, Epstein used the press to his advantage, playing willful scribes and tepid publishers.

———

With so much known about Epstein, it is almost unbelievable to imagine that for years he was able to get a pass from the media. So how did he do it? He paid for it. Literally.

On October 2, 2013, well after he had been publicly humiliated as a child sex predator, the financial magazine and website *Forbes* wrote a hagiographical item about him—mentioning none of his follies.

The piece was titled "Science Funder Jeffrey Epstein Launches Radical Emotional Software for the Gaming Industry" and detailed an artificial intelligence group behind changing game programming through new emotive software.[6] The first two-thirds of the article was semi-technical fluff, in praise of the company doing the work with Hong Kong researchers and government support. Then came the praise.

"Over the last ten years, Jeffrey Epstein has become one of the largest backers of cutting edge science around the world," claimed the article. The financier, the article continued, "has donated up to $200 million a year to eminent scientists." The statistic was falsely attributed to *New York* magazine. (It's unlikely he ever donated that much money in his lifetime, let alone on an annual basis.) Epstein's ties to Harvard were mentioned, then more highly inflated claims about his generosity.

The interesting thing about the supposed journalistic look at cutting-edge video game technology was that it was written by Epstein or his PR team. The author, Drew Hendricks, would admit in 2019 in an interview with *The New York Times* that he had received $600 to publish the article, which had been written for him.

And *Forbes* was not the only publication to fall for the ruse. Similar articles had appeared in *National Review* and *HuffPost*. The offending articles would be removed only after reporter inquiries in 2019.

It was all part of Epstein's plan: by throwing his money around, he could get his way. Just as he had in so many other avenues of his life.

—

In 2002, *Vanity Fair* reporter Vicky Ward would set out to examine Epstein's rise as a supposed money manager and political player following his trip to Africa with Bill Clinton. Ward's piece, published in 2003, would be important; it would frame Epstein as a major player, a man of mystery, and a confidence man.

But, according to Ward, she was not able to tell the whole story. She had information on "the girls." Not nearly the full extent that is known today, but enough that publication would have severely damaged the predator just as he was getting his wings.

Ward detailed the accusations she had in a 2015 *Daily Beast* article recalling how it all went down.[7] "Three on-the-record stories from a family: a mother and her daughters who came from Phoenix. The oldest daughter, an artist whose character was vouchsafed to me by several sources, including the artist Eric Fischl, had told me, weeping as she sat in my living room, of how Epstein had attempted to seduce both her and, separately, her younger sister, then only 16," she wrote.

The subject of her profile inquired about what she knew, and when he discovered the truth, he went ballistic. "Just the mention of a 16-year-old girl . . . carries the wrong impression. I don't see what it adds to the piece. And that makes me unhappy," Epstein told Ward.

He also called the powerful editor of *Vanity Fair*, Graydon Carter, who held final say over what was published in his magazine. Then he started sending "fabricated fakes" supposedly debunking the on-the-record accusations. And finally he visited the offices of *Vanity Fair*, while Ward was away on maternity leave. "By now everyone at the magazine was completely spooked," Ward recalls more than a decade and a half later.

Just before it was time for publication, Ward's direct editor delivered the message: "Graydon's taking out the women from the piece." Ward was in tears and furious.

"I began to cry. It was so wrong," Ward wrote later. "The family had been so brave."

She went to Carter to plead her case. "Why?"

"He's sensitive about the young women," Graydon Carter allegedly replied. "And we still get to run most of the piece."

Ward recalls, "It came down to my sources' word against Epstein's . . . and at the time Graydon believed Epstein. In my notebook I have him saying, 'I believe him.'"

In a statement responding to Ward's allegations, Carter said, "Epstein denied the charges at the time and since the claims were unsubstantiated and no criminal investigation had been initiated, we decided not to include them in what was a financial story."

—

Epstein fancied himself somewhat of a media mogul. At least that's what he aspired to be.

In 2003, he tried to buy *New York* magazine. Joining forces with heavy hitters from across media, Hollywood, and advertising, Epstein sought to have greater control over those who buy ink by the barrel. The group comprised the movie mogul Harvey Weinstein, the advertising executive Donny Deutsch, the moneyman Nelson Peltz, the journalist Michael Wolff, and the owner of *U.S. News & World Report*, Mort Zuckerman.

New York had written the first major profile of Epstein—a long, mostly laudatory piece that came out on the heels of his Africa trip. It had in some ways changed his trajectory. He had before that been only a slight fascination of gossip pages. But no longer.

It showed him firsthand the power of the press. And made him want a piece of it.

He, Deutsch, Peltz, Wolff, and Zuckerman put in an offer for the magazine for $44 million. It was somewhat of a lowball offer for the publication with a circulation of 440,000. Two others would bid more, and the winner would be the Wall Streeter Bruce Wasserstein, who ponied up $55 million.

In truth, all the bids would be too high from strictly a business view; *New York* made an annual profit of only $1 million. But it illustrates that the interest was never financial. The goal was power.

"These kind of players like to continually prove they are vital," the Yale School of Management associate dean Jeffrey A. Sonnenfeld told David Carr of *The New York Times*.[8] "What was motivating this deal was not a good financial outcome, but a demonstration of power. If it was no big deal, they would not have gotten involved in the first place."

Wolff, a good friend of Epstein's who was the original organizer of the group, admitted the error was teaming up with others. "We got outplayed . . . The idea of bringing together many interested parties seemed like a good idea, until it turned out to be a bad idea. It was less efficient than doing it with just one guy."

The failure, however, would leave Epstein undeterred. So the next year he joined forces with Zuckerman to invest $25 million in *Radar Magazine*. Epstein entered the enterprise an equal partner with Zuckerman but was a complete neophyte in terms of being in the publishing world.

But, at least outwardly, he took a business approach to the acquisition. "When I invest in companies, I invest in the people, and I don't think that anybody has the track record with start-ups that Mort does," Epstein told *The New York Times* in 2004.[9]

"I always focus on the potential downside of an investment, and I don't think this is something that is going to lose money," he added.

That last comment would perhaps show more hubris than knowledge. The magazine was an embarrassing flop.

Radar Magazine lasted only three issues.

"It's too difficult a climate to start magazines in, given the advertising conditions for this period of time," Zuckerman would tell *The New York Times*, publicly taking the fall for the financial failure.[10] Epstein did not publicly comment.

The blame would be placed squarely on advertising. It was a bust, they claimed, seemingly giving up before even giving it a serious chance for success.

But few close to the project believed that was the real reason. "No one could quite figure out why, after just three issues, after putting all that money in, they would suddenly abandon the project," *Radar*'s founding editor, Maer Roshan, told *Vanity Fair* in 2019.[11] "Our advertising revenue and circulation was far ahead of projections."

Roshan proposed a theory, however. "When you look at the sequence of events, it's clear that the police first approached Epstein at some point during the *Radar* rollout . . . It's not surprising that Mort [Zuckerman] would want to distance himself from that partnership as quickly as possible."

—

One of the ways Jeffrey Epstein played the press was by holding information over them—signaling that he knew damaging information about the rich and famous. And also by keeping them close. The story told by the *New York Times* journalist James B. Stewart illustrates this.

The journalist had contacted Epstein to determine whether he was advising Elon Musk, the founder of the electric car giant Tesla. The reporter had heard this was the case.

Musk's and his company's position would be clear—that it didn't happen. "It is incorrect to say that Epstein ever advised Elon on anything," a spokeswoman said.

But if one reads between the lines, the spokeswoman's denial is weak. It does not state, for instance, that Epstein and Musk never had conversations or that there was never a relationship. It rather slyly claims only that Musk never received advice from the predator.

Regardless of the Musk-Epstein relationship, it's a window into Epstein's operation. The reporter reached out to Epstein for comment, and instead received an invitation to his palatial New York mansion.

Stewart says he was greeted at the door by a young woman with an eastern European accent who led him upstairs, where he was soon joined by a casually dressed Epstein.

Epstein showed off his photos with world leaders, pointing to one of the crown prince of Saudi Arabia, Mohammed bin Salman, Woody Allen, and Bill Clinton.

They then began to chat. For an hour and a half.

The conversation was not limited to the work Epstein might have been doing for Tesla. Epstein, it appears, was keen to keep up the perception that he indeed was doing something for the car company and tech entrepreneur, but he also acknowledged that because of his reputation no one wanted to be associated with him. He predicted any such claim would be denied.

But of course a tie to a legitimate company—especially one like Tesla, which is seen as cutting-edge and in a major growth industry—served Epstein well. He would welcome any such association because it would make him seem perhaps more legitimate than he actually was.

A week after the interview, Stewart received a call from Epstein to see if he would join him for dinner together with his good buddy Woody Allen. Later he'd be invited to another Epstein dinner with the journalist Michael Wolff and the former Trump adviser Steve Bannon.

And then came the final offer: an invitation to Stewart to write a biography of Epstein. The journalist declined.

Nevertheless, the stunt Epstein tried to pull is reminiscent of a Jack Abramoff trick.

Abramoff, the prominent Washington, D.C., lobbyist who pleaded guilty in 2006 to tax evasion, conspiracy, and fraud, would try to win over staffers on Capitol Hill by offering them future jobs. The minute the jobs were accepted, the staffers no longer were working for the constituents but were, in effect, extensions of Abramoff's own lobbying shop.

"When we would become friendly with an office and they were important to us, and the chief of staff was a competent person, I would say or my staff would say to him or her at some point, 'You know, when you're done working on the Hill, we'd very much like you to consider coming to work for us,'" Abramoff revealed in an interview he gave to CBS's *60 Minutes* after he served three years in prison.[12]

He continued, "Now the moment I said that to them or any of our staff said that to 'em, that was it. We owned them. And what does that mean? Every request from our office, every request of our clients, everything that we want, they're gonna do. And not only that, they're gonna think of things we can't think of to do."

Surely Abramoff and Epstein did not operate in the same profession—one a lobbyist, the other a supposed money manager. But they worked in the same field. Both courted influence and wielded power, and used people as pawns in their quests to achieve their own goals. The notion that Epstein would try to strike an agreement favorable to the reporter seems reflective of his own true intentions in holding that meeting and the subsequent conversations.

16
The Arrest

The End Is Near

> *Mr. Epstein knew an astonishing number of rich, famous and powerful people, and had photos to prove it. He also claimed to know a great deal about these people, some of it potentially damaging or embarrassing, including details about their supposed sexual proclivities and recreational drug use.*
>
> **JAMES B. STEWART**

Jeffrey Epstein inhaled his last breath of free air on July 6, 2019. Arriving on a private jet at New Jersey's Teterboro Airport, the six-foot, 185-pound, now nearly all-white-haired sex predator would be picked up by federal authorities as his plane landed, arriving from Paris, France.

He'd be fingerprinted and processed, eventually moved by the federal government to the Metropolitan Correctional Center in Manhattan. He would never walk free again.

Federal records would reveal he'd been traveling with a Virgin

Islands driver's license, a Florida driver's license, an American Express card, a UnitedHealthcare insurance card, a Medicare insurance card, a U.S. Customs and Border Protection boaters option card, and a passport. He would check in no personal belongings to MCC.

The investigation of Epstein was being conducted by the federal prosecutors out of the Southern District of New York. But that was not the only federal law enforcement body pursuing charges. The U.S. Marshals Service was looking into whether he had filed his travel arrangements properly in accordance with laws surrounding registered sex offenders, which he had been since his first guilty plea in Florida more than a decade earlier.

The charges Epstein had been brought in on were related to activities between 2002 and 2005. He was being accused of sex trafficking of underage victims in New York and Florida. The charging documents said there were dozens of victims. And, as Epstein had been known to do, the victims had allegedly been paid off in cash.

The strange thing about the charges is that they did not cover more recent activities. And they appeared to piggyback off the earlier investigation into Epstein, which had of course resulted in his early guilty plea on state charges. It would not take Johnnie Cochran to envision that Epstein's defense—and who wouldn't have assumed there would be one?—would revolve around both a prior non-prosecution agreement he had signed with the feds in Florida and constitutional double-jeopardy questions.

The attorney general of the United States, Bill Barr, the son of the man who likely hired Epstein at Dalton so many years earlier, would say that his co-conspirators were likewise being investigated. The so-called co-conspirators would remain uncharged and unnamed as of the time of this writing, despite there being ample evidence that Epstein had assistance in carrying out his crimes.

Flight records of Epstein's plane would indicate that he had gone to Monaco and Austria, according to *The New York Times*.[1] Sex offenders are legally required to alert authorities of their whereabouts and travel arrangements, but he alerted authorities only that he was traveling to France and the Virgin Islands. Big-time criminals who are successful at evading the law have been known to be picked up on far more minor crimes, but the U.S. Marshals Service had not made an arrest on these apparent illegal actions.

More worrisome, girls were suspected of being aboard Epstein's plane throughout his 2019 international travel.

For the last few years, Epstein had been keeping a low profile. It had, until very recently, served him quite well. He had in a prior life flown too close to the sun. "It's the Icarus story, someone who flies too close to the sun," a reporter once told Epstein, giving him the elevator pitch on the story he was writing about the sex predator.

"Did Icarus like massages?" Epstein responded, making a self-deprecating crack.[2]

The wealth and power he had so aggressively sought had helped him achieve his ultimate ambitions. He had come a world away from the childhood he despised in the working-class confines of Coney Island. His friendships with world leaders and business titans gave him prestige. His philanthropy won him accolades from the top scholars and scientists of his generation. And it helped him carry out his business, which most assuredly was not—and never was— money management. But he had flown too close to the sun. He got burned.

This was not lost on him. "If my ultimate goal was to stay private, traveling with Clinton was a bad move on the chessboard. I recognize that now. But you know what? Even Kasparov makes them. You move on," he reportedly told a friend.[3]

His predatory ways were known. He was toxic.

And yet, in 2019, he was still going strong. Until his final arrest, he had not been stopped from continuing to traffic children, both for his sexual pleasure and for service of those still around him.

"Epstein engaged in a pattern and practice of trafficking and sexually abusing young women and female children on this private, secluded island of Little St. James where Epstein and his associates could avoid detection of their illegal activity from Virgin Islands and federal law enforcement and prevent these young women and underage girls from leaving freely and escaping the abuse," the U.S. Virgin Islands prosecutor Denise George would allege in a lawsuit filed in 2020 after his death.[4]

In fact, he had recently purchased, in 2016, another island, Great St. James, to help conceal these activities, the prosecutor asserted. The nearby island, divided up into three parcels valued together at nearly $23 million, allowed him "to further shield his conduct on Little St. James from view, prevent his detection by law enforcement of the public, and allow him to continue and conceal his criminal enterprise."

Moreover, according to the prosecutor, Epstein's intent was to expand his operation. The island provided not only privacy but also more land on which to carry out his crimes.

"The Epstein Enterprise maintained and made available young women and underage girls for the purpose of engaging them in forced

labor and sexual activities and used coercion and deception to procure, abuse, and harbor its victims."

This criminal activity occurred until his arrest in 2019, according
to the lawsuit. The number of girls involved is unknown. But it is believed that they may have been as young as twelve years old.

One fifteen-year-old tried to escape the sex enslavement by swim-
ming off the island, the lawsuit claimed. (A search party organized by
Epstein located her, detained her, and took away her passport.) Another girl who allegedly tried to escape was threatened with "physical
restraint of harm."

So how was Epstein able to still do it, despite being widely known
as a pariah? Because he was also still known as a mover and shaker.
His prior associations with the rich and powerful were still being used,
despite his new pariah status.

"The Epstein Enterprise deceptively lured underage girls and women
into its sex trafficking ring with money and promises of employment,
career opportunities and school assistance. The Epstein Enterprise
preyed on their financial and other vulnerabilities, and promised victims, money, shelter, gifts, employment, tuition and other items of value."

Besides, the girls were told, they were just being asked to give the
man a "massage."

It was, until the end, the same con Epstein had employed for decades.

—

Teterboro is the closest private airport to Manhattan. It caters to the
rich and famous, especially those with their own airplanes, offering

privacy and accessibility to high-status customers. It's only twelve miles away, making it convenient for the rich and famous to land their private jets and get into the city in under thirty minutes. That summer morning, Epstein was headed to his home in New York City.

So why did Epstein even return to the United States? Some have speculated that toward the end he lived his life in fear. That his scheme of treating world elites to forbidden—and illegal—goods was coming to an end.

The recent attention to Epstein, which began when the media started to reexamine his sweetheart deal cut by the then prosecutor Alex Acosta, had started taking a toll on his lifestyle and business interests. Deutsche Bank, which had had a long relationship with Epstein, began to examine his finances and seek distance. He reportedly had dozens of accounts with the German-based bank, and had borrowed money from the financial giant. His relationship with the bank reportedly was so complex that it had a hard time cutting him off completely; it was apparently too difficult a task to close all his accounts because not all his accounts were easily identifiable as his own.

Nevertheless, liquidity and borrowing began to get more difficult for him. And he had already been shut out of banks before.

"He had been a client of JPMorgan's private-banking division from the late 1990s until around 2013, five years after he had pleaded guilty to state prostitution charges," *The New York Times* reported.[5]

But with the renewed attention to Epstein—first the *Miami Herald* pieces, then a tsunami of more critical and probing coverage—Deutsche Bank made the calculation that it was more damaging to its profits to keep him as a client than it would be to cut him off entirely.

There was also widespread speculation among the financial community that Epstein had for years engaged in money laundering. No one could quite nail down how it was that he made his money, so certainly all profitable and even criminal enterprises remained possibilities. Deutsche Bank had its own theories. Wall Streeters in particular have long been keen to make these assumptions. The bank, it turned out, had similar concerns.

"In 2015 and 2016, anti-money laundering compliance officers in Deutsche Bank's offices in New York and Jacksonville, Fla., raised a variety of concerns about the work the bank was doing with Mr. Epstein," the *Times* reported.

"In addition, the compliance officers on at least one occasion noticed potentially illegal activity in one of Mr. Epstein's accounts, including transactions in which money was moving outside the United States, two of the people said. The compliance officers produced a so-called suspicious activity report, but it is unclear whether the report was ever filed with the Treasury Department's financial-crimes division."

These matters of internal concern were not enough to cut him off, however. "Despite the compliance officers' misgivings, the bank continued to do extensive business with Mr. Epstein," the paper said.

The bank was willing to work with Epstein as long as it didn't become public knowledge.

Which perhaps explains the somewhat dire straits Epstein found himself in in the summer of 2019. Because while it is obviously true that he had enough money to last him the rest of his life, it does not do anyone much good if he either cannot access that money or has to store it in his mattress.

Multiple sources who spent time with Epstein said they saw indications that he and Maxwell were collecting compromising material on their powerful circle of friends, either for their own private interests, for blackmail, or as part of a spy operation. Some of these impressions might have been due to Epstein's self-aggrandizement. He openly encouraged speculation that he was involved with intelligence agencies.

The friend said Epstein would also darkly hint that he had done work with the Central Intelligence Agency headquarters in Langley, Virginia.

"He would occasionally make mentions of, 'Well, in Langley they say . . . '" said the friend in an interview. "I don't know what that was about."

Laura Goldman, the friend of Ghislaine's, said she believes that if there was a spy operation, then it was orchestrated by Ghislaine rather than Epstein, due to her foreign government contacts.

"I really do think it was a spying operation," said Goldman. "I think the world is sexist, and they think it was [Epstein in charge]. It was always [Ghislaine]. She's the one with all the contacts; she's the one that organized everything."

"I think that she sold to the highest bidder," she added. "I don't know if she was as devoted to Israel as [her father, Robert Maxwell] was. So, I'm not sure that it all went to Israel. Some of it may have gone to MI6, and other places."

Epstein often played up his involvement with foreign government officials. He told one friend that he provided financial services to the crown prince of Saudi Arabia. (A source close to the Saudi government denied that Epstein provided financial advice to the crown prince but said he did travel to the country on business.)

When Epstein's Manhattan home was raided by the feds in 2019, they found that he had an Austrian passport that listed a fake name and an address in Saudi Arabia, which he allegedly used in the 1980s.

Epstein also had a close relationship with the former Israeli prime minister Ehud Barak.

"I saw Ehud Barak at his house. I think [he met him] through business; they had some kind of financial dealings together," said Epstein's former attorney Dershowitz in an interview. "I remember one day I went to his house for a meeting, and on the board was a map of the Middle East, hand drawn. [Epstein] said that was drawn by Ehud Barak and it was his idea for how to resolve the Palestine-Israel conflict. That was interesting to see."

But Dershowitz said he saw no evidence that Epstein was involved in any sort of intelligence activity.

"That's bullshit. That's just total bullshit. There were rumors around all the time, but he never worked for any intelligence," said Dershowitz. "The rumor comes from the fact that he was close to Ghislaine Maxwell, and Ghislaine's father, Robert Maxwell, was rumored to have worked for Mossad. I can't imagine that any intelligence agency would hire Jeffrey Epstein; I just don't think that's possible. I don't think he would fit the profile of who you get to work as an intelligence agent at any time. But who knows?"

———

Another unanswered mystery around Epstein is why he decided to return that fateful day in July, when the feds were waiting to place him under arrest. As one plugged-in source said, "He obviously decided it was worse to stay in Paris than to come back to New York. Right? Why would it be worse to be in Paris than in New York? Probably because he thought, after Khashoggi, whatever services he had been providing for Saudis, he was probably concerned that he might get dipped in acid, like Khashoggi. So he came back to New York to take his chances knowing that he'd be immediately arrested."

Jamal Khashoggi of course was the *Washington Post* columnist who was murdered inside a Saudi consulate in Turkey. He had entered the consulate to get paperwork necessary for his upcoming nuptials but had been brutally murdered and then allegedly dissolved in an acid substance so that his body could be carried out of the diplomatic posting without attention. The plot worked in part; he never walked out of there alive. But the Saudis got caught, and international uproar ensued.

The source wondered whether Epstein feared a similar fate. "That's where it gets back to this whole idea of he was providing services to Saudis and Iranians, whoever else he was providing. I mean it's taboo everywhere, but it's especially taboo over there. And so they have a lot of money," the source added.

Speaking of the whole Epstein scheme of providing young kids for the sexual pleasure of world elites, the source added, "He expanded his geography." Operating in the United States alone, to an American clientele, might no longer have been viable, while operating abroad, in foreign lands, provided endless opportunities, if perhaps extrajudicial risks.

A good friend of Epstein's recalled in an interview a discussion he had about Saudi Arabia. The friend recalled asking Epstein for advice about the famously reclusive country before a visit.

"What do you think about me going to Saudi Arabia?" the friend asked Epstein.

"Oh, they're going to cheat you and stab you in the back," Epstein replied.

"Did you have this experience?"

"Oh yeah," Epstein claimed. "I went to Saudi Arabia and the king wouldn't let me fly my own plane, I had to fly on his plane, and so when I got there, they put me at the Marriott and they kicked every other person out of the Marriott because they didn't want anyone else to have to stay with a Jew."

—

Moreover, there was further cause for concern when the feds discovered cash, diamonds, and an Austrian passport in the raid. Epstein certainly had motive and means to flee the country.

"Just this morning, the government became aware of a safe that contained a pile of cash, diamonds, a passport from a foreign country with a picture of the defendant under another name," Alex Rossmiller, an assistant U.S. attorney, said in court.[6]

"The passport was issued in the name of a foreign country, it was issued in the 1980s, it is expired, it shows a picture of Jeffrey Epstein, and another name," Rossmiller added.

Even more disturbing, as Epstein's lawyers negotiated with state prosecutors over a deal, it became clear that he was unwilling to accept any real restrictions on his interactions with young women and children as part of a settlement agreement. His attorneys quibbled with prosecutors over a clause that would bar Epstein from interacting with minors without a state-approved adult supervisor. Epstein also asked for a special exception regarding his "goddaughter"—one of Eva and Glenn Dubin's daughters, who was eleven years old at the time.

"I need to confirm that Mr. Epstein may be with his goddaughter without supervision," wrote Epstein's lawyer Guy Fronstin in the April 16, 2006, letter to state prosecutors.

Epstein had a "fixation" with his goddaughter and displayed a nude photograph of her as a young child in his home, one of his friends recalled in an interview.

"Suddenly there was a picture of a naked four year old . . . I said what the hell is that about, on the wall? He said that's my goddaughter. He had some fixation with the goddaughter," said the friend in an interview.

"That put it together for me. Having a picture of a naked girl on the wall is bizarre . . . It wasn't a sexual picture, but she didn't have any pants on."

U.S. District Court Judge Richard Berman, who was overseeing the case, found the prosecution's argument compelling. Despite Epstein's offer to put up an astronomical $100 million bond, his bail request would be denied. He was deemed a flight risk and repeat offender likely to harm kids if he were ever to walk free again.

"The crimes Mr. Epstein has been charged with are among the most heinous in the law principally, in the court's view, because they involve minor girls," Berman declared.[7]

"Mr. Epstein's alleged excessive attraction to sexual conduct with or in the presence of minor girls—which is said to include his soliciting and receiving massages from young girls and young women perhaps as many as four times a day—appears likely to be uncontrollable," he added. "It seems fair to say that Mr. Epstein's future behavior will be consistent with past behavior."

This time Epstein's stay in lockup would be different. And this time he would not get out alive.

CONCLUSION
Conspiracy

Epstein was hiding in plain sight. We all knew about him.

CINDY MCCAIN

There are many reasons not to believe the official account of Epstein's death. We don't need to know what happened to know we've probably been lied to.

We were told there was nothing to see on footage taken outside his cell only to be told later that the footage didn't exist. The death scene, which protocol requires be vigorously maintained so that investigations can be performed, was quickly touched. One expects in the case of a suicide to find the death tool on the person who killed himself or at the very least nearby. Nowhere in the coroner's report was a tool that could have killed Epstein chronicled. The guards mysteriously did not do their jobs, the cameras mysteriously did not work, and the coroner changed her findings without additional evidence.

Perhaps these are all coincidences.

Perhaps not.

It is easy to say that many benefited from his being dead. After all, now he cannot reveal the secrets. He cannot release the reams of blackmail footage he kept. He cannot speak from the grave.

The stories that did emerge after his death did damage to the fortunes and reputations of many of the rich and powerful. Bankers like the Barclays CEO, Jes Staley, came under investigation by their own companies for their relationship with Epstein. Tech titans, like Bill Gates, Facebook's CEO, Mark Zuckerberg, and LinkedIn's CEO, Reid Hoffman, were all revealed to have varying degrees of friendship with the admitted sexual predator.

Others fell from grace. The director of the MIT Media Lab, Joi Ito, was forced to leave his post over the donations he accepted from Epstein. The billionaire Leslie Wexner's career came to an unceremonious end when it was announced on February 20, 2020, that he would no longer be the CEO of L Brands and that a majority stake of Victoria's Secret would be sold off.[1] Another billionaire, Glenn Dubin, announced his own retirement just a couple of weeks earlier. "This Epstein thing has been toxic for him," the *New York Post* reported a hedge fund manager as saying.[2]

There are no doubt others whose secrets are still hidden, either in that cache of photos or elsewhere.

It's clear that Epstein would do anything to keep the power he had wanted his whole life. Maybe someone even more powerful than Epstein decided that allowing him to live was more of a risk than arranging for his death. There are plenty of other theories, and certainly some that haven't even been thought of yet.

It's only fair to say, however, that we will probably never know the true story in full. The reason for this is simple. Consider this question: Who would you believe to tell you what happened? The elite, the press, our political leaders, or law enforcement? These are the institutions every American has been told since childhood that can and should be trusted, because they have the best interests of all people at heart. But these are the very same institutions that shielded Jeffrey Epstein for years.

Epstein hobnobbed with the people who ran these institutions for years, even after his crimes were known. Go back through the archives of *The Palm Beach Post*, recall the blaring 2011 headline in the *New York Post* labeling Epstein a "perv," reread the litany of evidence in the pages of *The New York Times* and *The Wall Street Journal*. His scumminess had never escaped the reporters and editors at the broadsheets and tabloids. Epstein was known. His actions were no secret.

Cindy McCain, the wife of the late senator John McCain, admitted as much in a January 2020 public appearance. "Epstein was hiding in plain sight," she said at the State of the World 2020 Conference in Florida.[3] "We all knew about him. We all knew what he was doing, but we had no one that was—no legal aspect that would go after him. They were afraid of him. For whatever reason, they were afraid of him."

McCain would add that an Epstein victim went to school with one of her own children. "I hope he's in hell right now," she said.

And yet because Epstein was rich, because his friends were powerful, and, perhaps most important, because he had beaten the law before, it seemed as if he would get away with his crimes forever. At least that seems to have been his plan.

Epstein was made by the elites and for the elites. The wealthy helped him along every step of the way, and they shielded him during his life. It's unlikely that many of them would have an unbiased story of the truth—or would reveal if a member of their circle had bumped him off to prevent more stories from coming to light. And what reason do we have to trust those who said nothing about him during his life but now gossip about him now?

Epstein also had used the media to his advantage—appearing like a savior and using his new celebrity position to better ingratiate himself with the Upper East Side crowd he so craved to be a part of. Could we ever trust the people who kept up fawning coverage of this monster for years to tell us what "really happened" in the last moments of his life?

And then, of course, there were our leaders. To most of us they held exalted titles, by election or by birth. To Jeffrey Epstein they were powerful political connections that he carefully collected. Presidents and royalty were in his Rolodex. They took his money and in turn bestowed respect and reverence on him, the kind of legitimacy that only comes with a warm welcome into eminent institutions like the Trilateral Commission and the Council on Foreign Relations. And they also gave him their most limited resource—time. And as that time went on, it was they who seemed to need him. He was always ready with a private plane to help out a friend, or an invitation to an exotic locale, or a luxurious mansion or private island offered up for an intimate getaway. The horrifying nature of that intimacy—and the need for all the privacy—would become apparent only later, after much downplaying and stonewalling. Should we now believe Epstein's powerful friends when they tell us what happened to him?

Even law enforcement, whose mission is to treat everyone as equal before the law, was happy to take his contributions and use them—for what? To fight the worst in society? When it came time to investigate Epstein, they would cut him the sweetest of sweetheart deals. And while they were at it, they'd leak every step of the investigation to the perp himself so he'd have a heads-up of what was coming his way well before anything went down. But now their accounts of this high-profile criminal's demise are supposed to be accepted without question?

Epstein's crime wave was not some outside attack on our collective sense of decency. It was something worse—an inside job. And one that could have been carried out only with a methodical, slow-burning plan and lots and lots and lots of help.

But whatever happened to Epstein, one irony is clear: Epstein, the man who recorded everyone, failed to record his final act.

So, no, of course we cannot rely on the media, academics, politicians, or law enforcement to tell us simply that Epstein offed himself alone in a federal holding cell. These are the same people who harbored one of the worst homegrown terrorists America has ever produced.

And now we are left grappling with the insane story of Jeffrey Epstein, his life and his death, the shattered lives touched by his web of depravity, and one horrible lingering question: How many more like him did he leave behind?

ACKNOWLEDGMENTS

I t is especially difficult to write a book in mere months and on a topic continually breaking, often altering various story lines and reporting paths. That was predictable when we signed up for the gig.

But the story of Jeffrey Epstein was too important to pass up. The story of a great con with explosive and criminal deviance, entrapping America's most coveted and reviled class. At the time of his death, Epstein was perhaps the most hated man in America. His reputation has not gotten better, nor will it. And in the end the story is much worse and more pernicious than even we believed.

More than ever, we're cognizant of the people who suffered. Our hearts go out to Epstein's victims. We hope that by shedding light on at least a part of what they endured, and how Epstein did it, we'll be able to help them.

We could not have written *A Convenient Death* alone. We are very grateful to our editor, Bria Sandford, for coming up with this idea—and masterfully seeing it through. Bria is a joy to work with. And her steady hand and clear vision helped improve the manuscript, from start to finish. Thanks also to Nina Rodríguez-Marty.

Our agents, the team at Javelin, orchestrated this project from the get-go, putting us together and offering sage advice and thoughtful feedback. They were great. Special thanks to Keith Urbahn, Matt Latimer, and Dylan Colligan.

We are especially grateful to the sources who took time and energy to explain the inner workings of Epstein and his orbit. Some of them are named throughout the book. Others, for fear of reprisal, wished to remain anonymous. Even in death few dare to be associated with Epstein.

We would also like to thank the other reporters whose work we often relied on throughout this book. Their work was pioneering, often insightful, and ballsy. So thanks go to Vicky Ward, Julie K. Brown, William D. Cohan, James Patterson, John Connolly, Tim Malloy, Laura Goldman, Bob Fitrakis, Carol Felsenthal, Conchita Sarnoff, Nick Bryant, James B. Stewart, and many fine reporters and editors at the *Daily Beast*, the *New York Post*, *The New York Times*, and *The Wall Street Journal*.

And we're also grateful to our friends and colleagues who provided advice and feedback, especially Michael Goldfarb, Eliana Johnson, Aaron Harison, Victorino Matus, Matthew Continetti, and Rob Lockwood.

AG:

Big thanks to my co-author, Daniel Halper, a fantastic reporter and writer whose calmness under pressure helped keep me sane. It was a pleasure to work with and learn from him during this process.

I am grateful to my wonderful parents for their faith and encouragement. Thanks also to Josh, Dan, Muriel Post, Mark and Myra Goodman, and my editors Toby Harnden, Keith Koffler, and Hugo

Gurdon. Much gratitude goes to my friends and family who helped along the way, especially Karen Post, Katherine and Matt McCarty, Noah, Tom, John, Leslie, Stephen the Painter, and the amazing folks at Ocean Reef. Thanks to Jason for his friendship, love, and moral support.

DH:

I'm thankful for my co-author, Alana Goodman, who was just great to work with. She is an excellent and tenacious reporter. We were fortunate to see eye to eye every step of the way. That made everything smooth and even, dare I say, at times enjoyable.

My family provided support, never giving me too hard a time for missing events and holidays. Thanks especially to my wife, Lauren, who orchestrated all of it and did the heavy lifting. She's patient, forgiving, and especially wonderful. And my girls, Joanna, Eve, and Ruby, who provide bright light in a very dark world—and make everything worthwhile.

Thanks also to my parents, who always encourage me to keep writing; my in-laws, who are kind and generous; my brothers and their families; and Kimmy and Sam.

NOTES

EPIGRAPH

1. Julia Reinstein, "23 Women Stood in Court and Said Jeffrey Epstein Abused Them. Here Are Their Most Powerful Quotes," *BuzzFeed News*, Aug. 27, 2019, www.buzzfeednews.com/article/juliareinstein/jeffrey-epstein-women-victims-testify-court-quotes.

INTRODUCTION

1. Joe Pompeo, "Decoding Jeffrey Epstein's Mysterious, Star-Studded Black Book," *Vanity Fair*, July 18, 2019, www.vanityfair.com/news/2019/07/jeffrey-epstein-black-book-nick-bryant.
2. Tim Hains, "Julie K. Brown: 'Quite a Few Powerful and Important' Names Will Come Up in Jeffrey Epstein Sex Trafficking Case," RealClearPolitics, July 7, 2019, www.realclearpolitics.com/video/2019/07/07/julie_k_brown_quite_a _few_powerful_and_important_names_will_come_up_in_jeffrey_epstein _sex_trafficking_case.html.
3. Ellen Cranley, "Only 33% of Americans Believe That Jeffrey Epstein Actually Died by Suicide," *Business Insider*, Aug. 28, 2019, www.businessinsider.com /jeffrey-epstein-suicide-death-poll-2019-8.

CHAPTER 1: FINAL HOURS

1. Matthew Haag, "$56 Million Upper East Side Mansion Where Epstein Allegedly Abused Girls," *New York Times*, July 8, 2019, www.nytimes.com/2019/07 /08/nyregion/jeffrey-epstein-nyc-mansion.html.
2. Patricia Hurtado, Chris Dolmetsch, and Christian Berthelsen, "Jeffrey Epstein Joins 'El Chapo' in Notorious Jail as Inmate 76318-054," Bloomberg, July 10, 2019, www.bloomberg.com/news/articles/2019-07-10/epstein-joins-el-chapo-in -notorious-jail-as-inmate-76318-054.

3. Brooke Singman, "Jeffrey Epstein's Alleged Sex Trafficking Victim Named Bill Richardson, George Mitchell in Newly Released Documents," Fox News, Aug. 9, 2019, www.foxnews.com/politics/mitchell-richardson-accused.

4. Lia Eustachewich and Tamar Lapin, "Photos Show Bill Clinton, Ghislaine Maxwell on Epstein's 'Lolita Express' Jet," *New York Post*, Jan. 10, 2020, nypost .com/2020/01/09/photos-show-bill-clinton-ghislaine-maxwell-on-epsteins -lolita-express-jet/.

CHAPTER 2: A CORPSE ON 9-SOUTH

1. Kate Sheehy, "New Photos of Jeffrey Epstein's Body, Sheet He Used to 'Hang Himself,'" *New York Post*, Jan. 5, 2020, nypost.com/2020/01/05/new-photos-of -jeffrey-epsteins-body-sheet-he-used-to-hang-himself/.

2. docplayer.net/153402820-V-19-cr-490-rmb-new-york-n-y-august-27-30-a-m -hon-richard-m-berman-district-judge-appearances.html.

3. How to Become a Medical Examiner (Forensic Pathologist), YouTube, Totowa Broadcast News, 2016, www.youtube.com/watch?v=tlzy0MEc61o.

CHAPTER 3: STONEWALLING

1. Danielle Robay, *Epstein: Devil in the Darkness*, 2019, www.stitcher.com/podcast /endeavor-co/epstein-devil-in-the-darkness.

2. Michael Gold, Danielle Ivory, and Nicole Hong, "Guards Accused of Napping and Shopping Online the Night Epstein Died," *New York Times*, Nov. 19, 2019, www.nytimes.com/2019/11/19/nyregion/epstein-prison-guards-arrested .html.

3. Josh Russell, "Jeffrey Epstein Guards Charged in NY," Courthouse News Service, Nov. 19, 2019, www.courthousenews.com/jeffrey-epstein-guards-charged -in-ny/.

4. Pervaiz Shallwani and Pilar Melendez, "Indictment Against Jail Guards Reveals News Details from Jeffrey Epstein's Final Hours," *Daily Beast*, Nov. 19, 2019, www.thedailybeast.com/jeffrey-epstein-death-jail-guards-who-were -supposed-to-watch-him-on-day-of-suicide-are-charged.

5. Matt Zapotosky and Devlin Barrett, "Corrections Officers Did Not Check on Epstein for 'Several' Hours Before His Death, Violating Protocol, Person Familiar with Case Says," *Washington Post*, Aug. 11, 2019, www.washingtonpost .com/national-security/it-was-inevitable-officers-watching-epstein-were -on-overtime-due-to-jail-staffing-shortage-union-president-says/2019/08/11 /2b611404-bc5e-11e9-a5c6-1e74f7ec4a93_story.html.

6. Michael Balsamo and Michael R. Sisak, "AP Sources: Jail Guards at Time of Epstein Death Reject Deal," Associated Press, Nov. 16, 2019, apnews.com /11ae6142bbb84af49daae80b94f1b4e2.

7. Mark Hosenball, "FBI Studies Two Broken Cameras Outside Cell Where Epstein Died: Source," Reuters, Aug. 28, 2019, www.reuters.com/article/us -people-jeffrey-epstein-cameras/fbi-studies-two-broken-cameras-outside -cell-where-epstein-died-source-idUSKCN1VI2LC.

8. "Security Footage Confirms No One Entered Area Epstein Was Jailed the Night He Died, Attorney General Says," CNBC, Nov. 22, 2019, www.cnbc.com/2019 /11/22/no-one-entered-area-epstein-was-jailed-the-night-he-died-attorney -general-says.html.

9. Reis Thebault, "Video from Epstein's First Apparent Suicide Attempt Lost Due to 'Technical Errors,' Prosecutors Say," *Washington Post*, Jan. 9, 2020, www.washingtonpost.com/nation/2020/01/09/video-epsteins-first-apparent -suicide-attempt-lost-due-technical-errors-prosecutors-say/.

CHAPTER 4: WHAT HAPPENED

1. Adam Klasfeld, "Jail Where Epstein Died Has Record of Security Blunders," Courthouse News Service, Aug. 13, 2019, www.courthousenews.com/jail-where -epstein-died-has-record-of-security-blunders/.

2. Jeremy Diamond, "Trump Promotes Epstein-Clintons Conspiracy Theory, the Latest in a Pattern of Baseless Claims Spread by President," CNN, Aug. 11, 2019, www.cnn.com/2019/08/11/politics/jeffrey-epstein-trump-conspiracy-theory -clintons/index.html.

3. Michael Balsamo, "AG Barr: Epstein's Death Was a 'Perfect Storm of Screw-Ups,'" Associated Press, Nov. 22, 2019, apnews.com/4ff27f28f32d446795b65 ac7dd8cc4ac.

4. Lee Brown, "Famed Pathologist Michael Baden Says Jeffrey Epstein's Death Was Homicide," *New York Post*, Oct. 30, 2019, nypost.com/2019/10/30/famed -pathologist-michael-baden-says-jeffrey-epsteins-death-was-homicide/.

5. Melissa Leon, "Jeffrey Epstein's Autopsy More Consistent with Homicidal Strangulation Than Suicide, Dr. Michael Baden Reveals," Fox News, Oct. 30, 2019, www.foxnews.com/us/forensic-pathologist-jeffrey-epstein-homicide -suicide.

CHAPTER 5: BLACKMAIL

1. Larry Celona and Chris Perez, "Epstein Had Bizarre Painting of Bill Clinton in Dress, Heels in Townhouse," *New York Post*, Aug. 14, 2019, nypost.com

/2019/08/14/epstein-had-bizarre-painting-of-bill-clinton-in-dress-heels -in-townhouse/.

2. James B. Stewart, "The Day Jeffrey Epstein Told Me He Had Dirt on Powerful People," *New York Times*, Aug. 12, 2019, www.nytimes.com/2019/08/12 /business/jeffrey-epstein-interview.html.

3. "Jeffrey Epstein Accuser Maria Farmer Says Ghislaine Maxwell Threatened Her Life, FBI 'Failed' Her," CBS News, Nov. 19, 2019, www.cbsnews.com/news /jeffrey-epstein-accuser-maria-farmer-says-ghislaine-maxwell-threatened -her-life-after-assault-fbi-failed/.

4. Andrew Denney, Larry Celona, and Bruce Golding, "Feds Found 'Vast Trove' of Nude Photos in Jeffrey Epstein's Safe," *New York Post*, July 8, 2019, nypost.com /2019/07/08/feds-found-vast-trove-of-nude-photos-in-jeffrey-epsteins-safe/.

CHAPTER 6: ILL-GOTTEN GAINS

1. "Sea Gate—Brooklyn's Only Gated Community," The Brooklyn Hopper, Aug. 18, 2017, www.thebrooklynhopper.com/sea-gate-brooklyns-gated-community/.

2. James Patterson, John Connolly, and Tim Malloy, *Filthy Rich* (New York: Grand Central Publishing, 2017).

3. Jerry Lambe, "The 'Epstein-Barr' Problem of New York City's Dalton School," Law & Crime, July 13, 2019, lawandcrime.com/high-profile/the-epstein-barr -problem-of-new-york-citys-dalton-school/.

4. Cat Schuknecht, "A Young Jeffrey Epstein Made an Impression on His High School Students," NPR, July 19, 2019, www.npr.org/2019/07/19/742725946/a -young-jeffrey-epstein-made-an-impression-on-his-high-school-students.

5. Linda Robertson and Aaron Brezel, "'Poor, Smart, and Desperate to Be Rich': How Epstein Went from Teaching to Wall Street," *Miami Herald*, July 16, 2019, www.miamiherald.com/news/state/florida/article232678997.html.

6. Robertson and Brezel, "'Poor, Smart, and Desperate to Be Rich.'"

7. Patterson, Connolly, and Malloy, *Filthy Rich*.

8. Kate Briquelet, "When Epstein Was Cosmo's Bachelor of the Month," *Daily Beast*, July 28, 2019, www.thedailybeast.com/when-jeffrey-epstein-was -cosmopolitan-bachelor-of-the-month.

9. Patterson, Connolly, and Malloy, *Filthy Rich*.

10. Vicky Ward, "The Talented Mr. Epstein," *Vanity Fair*, March 2003, www .vanityfair.com/news/2003/03/jeffrey-epstein-200303.

11. Gregory Zuckerman and Khadeeja Safdar, "Epstein Flourished as He Forged Bond with Retail Billionaire," *Wall Street Journal*, July 12, 2019, www.wsj.com /articles/epstein-flourished-as-he-forged-bond-with-retail-billionaire -11562975711.

12. Brian Pascus and Mola Lenghi, "Jeffrey Epstein Worked at Financial Firm That Engaged in Massive Ponzi Scheme in 1980s and 1990s," CBS News, Aug. 13, 2019, www.cbsnews.com/news/jeffrey-epstein-worked-at-towers-financial -with-stephen-hoffenberg-who-committed-ponzi-scheme-crimes/.

13. Edward Jay Epstein, "My Tea with Jeffrey Epstein," *Air Mail*, Sept. 14, 2019, airmail.news/issues/2019-9-14/my-tea-with-jeffrey-epstein.

14. Kate Briquelet and Tracy Connor, "Ponzi Scheme Victims Say Epstein Swindled Them," *Daily Beast*, July 14, 2019, www.thedailybeast.com/did-jeffrey -epstein-help-steven-hoffenberg-swindle-dollar460-million-in-ponzi -scheme.

CHAPTER 7: THE ACCOMPLICE

1. Darrell Hofheinz, "Palm Beach House in the Spotlight in Epstein Case," *Palm Beach Post*, July 8, 2019, www.palmbeachpost.com/news/20190708/palm -beach-house-in-spotlight-in-epstein-case.

2. Joe Shute, "The Maxwell Dynasty: What Happened to the Disgraced Mogul's Family?," *Telegraph*, Aug. 14, 2019, www.telegraph.co.uk/family/life/maxwell -dynasty-happened-disgraced-moguls-family/.

3. Elisabeth Maxwell, *A Mind of My Own: My Life with Robert Maxwell* (New York: HarperCollins, 1994).

4. "The High Society That Surrounded Jeffrey Epstein," Intelligencer, *New York*, July 22, 2019, nymag.com/intelligencer/2019/07/jeffrey-epstein-high-society -contacts.html.

5. Emma Parry, "Epstein Pal Ghislaine Maxwell Milked Millionaire Dad's Connections & Threw Parties with Vodka on Ice & Seafood Banquets," *Sun*, Nov. 23, 2019, www.thesun.co.uk/news/10395886/epstein-madam-ghislaine -maxwell-milked-billionaire-dad-and-threw-lavish-parties-with-beautiful -women/.

6. Megan Twohey and Jacob Bernstein, "The 'Lady of the House' Who Was Long Entangled with Jeffrey Epstein," *New York Times*, July 15, 2019, www.nytimes .com/2019/07/15/us/ghislaine-maxwell-epstein.html.

7. www.sa15.state.fl.us/stateattorney/NewsRoom/_content/PublicRecords /Epstein/STATE%20FILE%20REDACTED%20AND%20RELEASED /JEFFREY%20EPSTEIN%20PART%2016%20REDACTED.pdf.

8. Emine Saner, "'She Was So Dangerous': Where in the World Is the Notorious Ghislaine Maxwell?," *Guardian*, Dec. 12, 2019, www.theguardian.com/us-news /2019/dec/12/she-was-so-dangerous-where-in-the-world-is-the-notorious -ghislaine-maxwell.

9. Saner, "'She Was So Dangerous.'"
10. Matthew Schneier, "Ghislaine Maxwell, the Socialite on Jeffrey Epstein's Arm," The Cut, New York, July 15, 2019, www.thecut.com/2019/07/ghislaine-maxwell-the-socialite-on-jeffrey-epsteins-arm.html.
11. Julie K. Brown, "How a Future Trump Cabinet Member Gave a Serial Sex Abuser the Deal of a Lifetime," Miami Herald, Nov. 28, 2018, www.miamiherald.com/news/local/article220097825.html.
12. Beth Reinhard et al., "'She Was Shaking': Court Filings Describe System Jeffrey Epstein Allegedly Used to Procure Girls," Washington Post, Aug. 9, 2019, www.washingtonpost.com/politics/she-was-shaking-court-filings-describe-system-jeffrey-epstein-allegedly-used-to-procure-girls/2019/08/09/83093f3e-babe-11e9-bad6-609f75bfd97f_story.html.

CHAPTER 8: THE VICTIMS

1. Lulu Ramadan, "Jeffrey Epstein Case: The 'Open Secret' at Royal Palm High," Palm Beach Post, July 26, 2019, www.palmbeachpost.com/news/20190726/jeffrey-epstein-case-open-secret-at-royal-palm-high.
2. Conchita Sarnoff, TrafficKing: The Jeffrey Epstein Case (New York: Simon & Schuster, 2020).

CHAPTER 9: THE PERPS

1. Sharon Churcher, "Prince Andrew and the 17-Year-Old Girl His Sex Offender Friend Flew to Britain to Meet Him," Daily Mail, March 2, 2011, www.dailymail.co.uk/news/article-1361039/Prince-Andrew-girl-17-sex-offender-friend-flew-Britain-meet-him.html.
2. Conchita Sarnoff, TrafficKing: The Jeffrey Epstein Case (New York: Simon & Schuster, 2020).
3. Lia Eustachewich, "'Sex Slave' Claims Bill Clinton Visited Epstein's 'Orgy Island,'" Page Six, January 24, 2015, https://pagesix.com/2015/01/24/sex-slave-claims-bill-clinton-visited-epsteins-orgy-island/.
4. "Private Properties," Wall Street Journal, April 18, 1997, www.wsj.com/articles/SB861139935702093000.
5. Ben Feuerherd and Emily Saul, "Creepy Phone Messages Revealed in Jeffrey Epstein Document Dump," New York Post, Aug. 9, 2019, nypost.com/2019/08/09/creepy-phone-messages-revealed-in-jeffrey-epstein-document-dump/.

6. Doe v. United States, Case No. 08-80736-CIV-MARRA, S.D. Fla., Sep. 16, 2019, https://www.dropbox.com/s/65bpx6kew9n7q27/Doe%20v.%20United%20States%20of%20America%20-%20291.pdf?dl=0.

7. Second Circuit U.S. Court of Appeals, Giuffre v. Maxwell, Case #0:18-Cv-02868, PacerMonitor, Sep. 28, 2018, www.pacermonitor.com/public/case/25805805/Giuffre_v_Maxwell.

8. Jeremy Roebuck, "Ex-U.S. Senator Accused in Jeffrey Epstein Scandal Oversaw Philly Archdiocese's Sex-Abuse Compensation Fund," *Philadelphia Inquirer*, Aug. 22, 2019, www.inquirer.com/news/jeffrey-epstein-george-mitchell-philly-archdiocese-sex-abuse-clergy-20190822.html.

9. Dan Mangan and Kevin Breuninger, "Court Releases Documents About Jeffrey Epstein, Accused in Sex Traffic Case, and His Alleged Procurer Ghislaine Maxwell," CNBC, Aug. 9, 2019, www.cnbc.com/2019/08/09/documents-released-about-jeffrey-epstein-and-ghislaine-maxwell.html.

10. Kate Briquelet et al., "Jeffrey Epstein Accuser Names Powerful Men in Alleged Sex Ring," *Daily Beast*, Aug. 9, 2019, www.thedailybeast.com/jeffrey-epstein-unsealed-documents-name-powerful-men-in-sex-ring.

11. Alan Dershowitz, *Guilt by Accusation: The Challenge of Proving Innocence in the Age of #MeToo* (New York: Skyhorse, 2019).

CHAPTER 10: HOW HE GOT AWAY THE FIRST TIME

1. Rob Wile and Aaron Brezel, "Jeffrey Epstein Doled Out Millions to Harvard and Others. Is That Cash Tainted?," *Miami Herald*, July 22, 2019, www.miamiherald.com/news/state/florida/article232966202.html.

2. archive.org/stream/6506517-Exhibits-Part-2-Recarey-Depo/6506517-Exhibits-Part-2-Recarey-Depo_djvu.txt.

3. litvenenko.blog/2019/08/15/the-relationship-between-jeffrey-epstein-bill-and-hillary-clinton-donald-trump-and-ghislaine-maxwell/.

4. Kara Scannell and Brynn Gingras, "Jeffrey Epstein Allegedly Hired Private Investigators to Stalk His Victims," CNN, July 12, 2019, www.cnn.com/2019/07/12/us/jeffery-epstein-witness-intimidation/index.html.

5. "Perversion of Justice: The Shocking Story of a Serial Sex Abuser & Trump's Sec. of Labor, Who Helped Him," Democracy Now!, Jan. 4, 2019, www.democracynow.org/2019/1/4/perversion_of_justice_the_shocking_story.

6. Pilar Melendez, Katie Baker, Tracy Connor, and Kate Briquelet, "Jeffrey Epstein Abused Victims While Serving Time in Florida, Accuser's Lawyer Says," *Daily Beast*, July 16, 2019, www.thedailybeast.com/jeffrey-epstein-abused-victims-while-serving-time-in-florida-lawyer-brad-edwards-says.

CHAPTER 11: THE PRINCE

1. Lee Brown, "Prince Andrew Openly Groped Girls on Jeffrey Epstein's 'Pedophile Island': Prosecutor," *New York Post*, Feb. 16, 2020, www.nypost.com /2020/02/16/prince-andrew-openly-groped-girls-on-jeffrey-epsteins -pedophile-island-prosecutor/.
2. Holly Aguirre, "U.S. Virgin Islands A.G. Outraged at Epstein Estate's Efforts to Control the Case," *Vanity Fair*, Feb. 13, 2020, www.vanityfair.com/news /2020/02/us-virgin-islands-ag-outraged-at-epstein-estate-efforts-to-control -case.
3. Charlie Gasparino, "Jeffrey Epstein Before He Died: 'The Only Thing Worse Than Being Called a Pedophile Is Being Called a Hedge Fund Manager': FOX BUSINESS EXCLUSIVE," Fox Business, Aug. 13, 2019, www.foxbusiness .com/features/jeffrey-epstein-exclusive-hedge-fund.
4. Edward Klein, "The Trouble with Andrew," *Vanity Fair*, Aug. 2011, archive .vanityfair.com/article/share/ac60f552-4163-4d39-a36b-d2014fe20062.
5. Jon Swaine, "Sarah Ferguson 'Continually on Verge of Bankruptcy,'" *Telegraph*, June 13, 2011, www.telegraph.co.uk/news/uknews/theroyalfamily/8571793 /Sarah-Ferguson-continually-on-verge-of-bankruptcy.html.
6. Virginia Roberts, "The Billionaire's Playboy Club," www.documentcloud.org /documents/6251258-Virginia-Roberts-Memoir.html/#document/p40.
7. "Prince Andrew Interview: Jeffrey Epstein Stay Was 'Wrong Thing to Do,'" BBC, Nov. 16, 2019, www.bbc.com/news/uk-50431163.
8. Cathy Burke, "Prince Andrew Tours Manhattan with Billionaire Sex Offender Jeffrey Epstein," *New York Post*, Feb. 21, 2011, nypost.com/2011/02/21/prince -andrew-tours-manhattan-with-billionaire-sex-offender-jeffrey-epstein/.
9. Tatiana Siegel and Marisa Guthrie, "Jeffrey Epstein Moved Freely in Hollywood Circles Even After 2008 Conviction," *Hollywood Reporter*, July 10, 2019, www.hollywoodreporter.com/news/jeffrey-epstein-moved-freely-hollywood -circles-2008-conviction-1223336.
10. "A Statement by His Royal Highness the Duke of York," Royal Family, Nov. 20, 2019, www.royal.uk/statement-his-royal-highness-duke-york.
11. Sara Nathan and Kate Sheehy, "Prince Andrew Refuses to Cooperate with Feds in Jeffrey Epstein Probe," *New York Post*, Jan. 27, 2020, nypost.com/2020 /01/27/prince-andrew-refuses-to-cooperate-with-feds-in-jeffrey-epstein -probe/.

CHAPTER 12: THE POLITICIAN

1. Terrence K. Williams (@w_terrence), "Died of SUICIDE on 24/7 SUICIDE WATCH ? Yeah right! How does that happen #JefferyEpstein had information

on Bill Clinton & now he's dead I see #TrumpBodyCount trending," Twitter, Aug. 10, 2019, 2:26 p.m., twitter.com/w_terrence/status/1160256105399967744.

2. Landon Thomas Jr., "Jeffrey Epstein: International Moneyman of Mystery," *New York*, Oct. 29, 2002, nymag.com/nymetro/news/people/n_7912/.

3. Alana Goodman, "Bill Clinton in 2001: 'I've Never Had More Money in My Life,'" *Washington Free Beacon*, Oct. 13, 2015, freebeacon.com/issues/bill -clinton-in-2001-ive-never-had-more-money-in-my-life/.

4. Taylor Nicole Rogers, "Here Are All the Politicians Jeffrey Epstein, the Money Manager Arrested on Charges of Sex Trafficking, Has Donated To," *Business Insider*, July 11, 2019, www.businessinsider.in/miscellaneous/here-are-all -the-politicians-jeffrey-epstein-the-money-manager-arrested-on-charges -of-sex-trafficking-has-donated-to/slidelist/70183512.cms.

5. Emily Shugerman and Suzi Parker, "Jeffrey Epstein Visited Clinton White House Multiple Times in Early '90s," *Daily Beast*, July 24, 2019, www.the dailybeast.com/jeffrey-epstein-visited-clinton-white-house-multiple -times-in-early-90s.

6. Shugerman and Parker, "Jeffrey Epstein Visited Clinton White House Multiple Times in Early '90s."

7. Pilar Melendez, "Bill Clinton Failed to Mention His Intimate 1995 Dinner with Epstein," *Daily Beast*, July 11, 2019, www.thedailybeast.com/bill-clinton -failed-to-mention-his-intimate-1995-dinner-with-epstein.

8. Angelo Fichera and Saranac Hale Spencer, "The Epstein Connections Fueling Conspiracy Theories," FactCheck.org, Aug. 15, 2019, www.factcheck.org/2019 /08/the-epstein-connections-fueling-conspiracy-theories/.

9. Carol Felsenthal, *Clinton in Exile: A President out of the White House* (New York: Harper, 2008).

10. Thomas, "Jeffrey Epstein: International Moneyman of Mystery."

11. Thomas, "Jeffrey Epstein: International Moneyman of Mystery."

12. Conchita Sarnoff, *TrafficKing: The Jeffrey Epstein Case* (New York: Simon & Schuster, 2020).

13. www.courthousenews.com/wp-content/uploads/2019/08/Giuffre-unseal.pdf.

14. Martha Ross, "Chelsea Clinton Denies She Was Ever Close Friends with Jeffrey Epstein's Alleged 'Madam,'" *Mercury News*, July 22, 2019, www.mercurynews .com/2019/07/22/chelsea-clinton-denies-she-was-ever-close-friends -with-jeffrey-epsteins-alleged-madam/.

15. Angel Ureña (@angelurena), "Statement on Jeffrey Epstein," Twitter, July 8, 2019, 6:27 p.m., twitter.com/angelurena/status/1148357927625023490?lang=en.

16. Jacob Bernstein, "Whatever Happened to Ghislaine Maxwell's Plan to Save the Oceans?," *New York Times*, Aug. 14, 2019, www.nytimes.com/2019/08/14 /style/ghislaine-maxwell-terramar-boats-jeffrey-epstein.html.

17. "Sustainable Oceans Alliance: Impacting the SGDs," Clinton Foundation, Dec. 22, 2016, www.clintonfoundation.org/clinton-global-initiative/commitments /sustainable-oceans-alliance-impacting-sgds.

18. Jodi Kantor and Megan Twohey, *She Said: Breaking the Sexual Harassment Story That Helped Ignite a Movement* (New York: Penguin, 2019).

19. Kat Tenbarge, "Trump Addresses Jeffrey Epstein Connection, Claims the Two Haven't Spoken in 15 Years After a 'Falling Out,'" *Business Insider*, July 9, 2019, www.businessinsider.com/trump-epstein-had-falling-out-havent-spoken -in-15-years-2019-7.

20. Annie Karni and Maggie Haberman, "Jeffrey Epstein Was a 'Terrific Guy,' Donald Trump Once Said. Now He's 'Not a Fan,'" *New York Times*, July 9, 2019, www.nytimes.com/2019/07/09/us/politics/trump-epstein.html.

21. Vicky Ward, "Jeffrey Epstein's Sick Story Played Out for Years in Plain Sight," *Daily Beast*, July 9, 2019, www.thedailybeast.com/jeffrey-epsteins-sick-story -played-out-for-years-in-plain-sight.

22. Julie K. Brown, "How a Future Trump Cabinet Member Gave a Serial Sex Abuser the Deal of a Lifetime," *Miami Herald*, Nov. 28, 2018, www.miami herald.com/news/local/article220097825.html.

23. Kevin Breuninger and Valerie Block, "Trump Labor Secretary Alex Acosta Resigns amid Pressure from Jeffrey Epstein Sex Traffic Case," CNBC, July 12, 2019, www.cnbc.com/2019/07/12/labor-secretary-alex-acosta-is-resigning-as -pressure-mounts-from-jeffrey-epstein-case.html.

24. Sara Nathan and Mara Siegler, "Jeffrey Epstein's Gal Pal Ghislaine Maxwell Spotted at In-N-Out Burger in First Photos Since His Death," *New York Post*, Aug. 16, 2019, nypost.com/2019/08/15/jeffrey-epsteins-gal-pal-ghislaine -maxwell-spotted-at-in-n-out-burger-in-first-photos-since-his-death/.

25. Terrence K. Williams (@w_terrence), "Died of SUICIDE on 24/7 SUICIDE WATCH ? Yeah right! How does that happen #JefferyEpstein had informa- tion on Bill Clinton & now he's dead I see #TrumpBodyCount trending," Twitter, Aug. 10, 2019, 2:26 p.m., twitter.com/w_terrence/status/11602561053 99967744.

26. Quint Forgey, "Trump Defends Sharing Clinton-Epstein Conspiracy The- ory," *Politico*, Aug. 13, 2019, www.politico.com/story/2019/08/13/trump-clinton -epstein-conspiracy-theory-1460646.

27. Kelsey Tamborrino, "Kellyanne Conway on Epstein's Death: Trump Wants Everything Investigated," *Politico*, Aug. 11, 2019, www.politico.com/story/2019 /08/11/jeffrey-epstein-kellyanne-conway-trump-clinton-1457217.

28. Rebecca Morin, "Spokesman: Bill Clinton 'Knows Nothing' About 'Terrible Crimes' Alleged Against Epstein," *USA Today*, July 8, 2019, www.usatoday

.com/story/news/politics/2019/07/08/bill-clinton-knows-nothing-jeffrey
-epsteins-alleged-crimes/1679345001/.

CHAPTER 13: EPSTEIN'S SECRET

1. Mary Hanbury, "Victoria's Secret Head Les Wexner Describes How He Met Convicted Sex Offender Jeffrey Epstein in a 500-Word Letter to Members of His Charitable Foundation," *Business Insider*, Aug. 8, 2019, www.businessinsider.com/les-wexner-describes-how-he-met-jeffrey-epstein-2019-8.
2. William D. Cohan, "How Jeffrey Epstein Got His Hooks into Les Wexner," *Vanity Fair*, Aug. 8, 2019, www.vanityfair.com/news/2019/08/how-jeffrey-epstein-got-his-hooks-into-les-wexner.
3. Cohan, "How Jeffrey Epstein Got His Hooks into Les Wexner."
4. Landon Thomas Jr., "Jeffrey Epstein: International Moneyman of Mystery," *New York*, Oct. 29, 2002, nymag.com/nymetro/news/people/n_7912/.
5. Hanbury, "Victoria's Secret Head Les Wexner Describes How He Met Convicted Sex Offender Jeffrey Epstein in a 500-Word Letter to Members of His Charitable Foundation."
6. int.nyt.com/data/documenthelper/1500-alicia-arden-police-report/04e6cef6 bfb8b25c8684/optimized/full.pdf.
7. Emily Steel et al., "How Jeffrey Epstein Used the Billionaire Behind Victoria's Secret for Wealth and Women," *New York Times*, July 25, 2019, www.nytimes.com/2019/07/25/business/jeffrey-epstein-wexner-victorias-secret.html.
8. "Jeffrey Epstein Accuser Maria Farmer Says Ghislaine Maxwell Threatened Her Life, FBI 'Failed' Her," CBS News, Nov. 19, 2019, www.cbsnews.com/news/jeffrey-epstein-accuser-maria-farmer-says-ghislaine-maxwell-threatened-her-life-after-assault-fbi-failed/.
9. Steel et al., "How Jeffrey Epstein Used the Billionaire Behind Victoria's Secret for Wealth and Women."
10. Joe Nocera, "More Questions About How Jeffrey Epstein Got Island-Owning Rich," Bloomberg, July 17, 2019, www.bloomberg.com/opinion/articles/2019-07-17/more-questions-about-how-jeffrey-epstein-got-island-owning-rich.
11. Mark Remillard, "Billionaire Businessman Leslie Wexner Refuses to Reveal Full Scope of Jeffrey Epstein's Alleged Multimillion-Dollar Theft," ABC News, Jan. 23, 2020, www.abcnews.go.com/US/billionaire-businessman-leslie-wexner-refuses-reveal-full-scope/story?id=68461262.
12. Julie Baumgold, "The Bachelor Billionaire: On Pins and Needles with Leslie Wexner," *New York*, Aug. 5, 1985.

CHAPTER 14: THE SMART SET

1. Leland Nally, "Jeffrey Epstein, My Very, Very Sick Pal," *Mother Jones*, Aug. 23, 2019, www.motherjones.com/crime-justice/2019/08/jeffrey-epstein-my-very-very-sick-pal/.

2. Robert M. Braceras, Jennifer L. Chunias, and Kevin P. Martin, "Report Concerning Jeffrey Epstein's Interactions with the Massachusetts Institute of Technology," Goodwin Procter LLP, Jan. 10, 2020, factfindingjan2020.mit.edu/files/MIT-report.pdf.

3. Emily Flitter and James B. Stewart, "Bill Gates Met with Jeffrey Epstein Many Times, Despite His Past," *New York Times*, Oct. 12, 2019, www.nytimes.com/2019/10/12/business/jeffrey-epstein-bill-gates.html.

4. Evgeny Morozov, "Jeffrey Epstein's Intellectual Enabler," *New Republic*, Aug. 22, 2019, newrepublic.com/article/154826/jeffrey-epsteins-intellectual-enabler.

5. Tyler Cowen, "The American Wealthy Have Been Redefining Social Status Through a Practice Known as 'Countersignaling,'" *Business Insider*, March 4, 2017, www.businessinsider.com/wearing-casual-clothes-at-work-to-show-wealth-2017-2.

6. Nally, "Jeffrey Epstein, My Very, Very Sick Pal."

7. James B. Stewart, Matthew Goldstein, and Jessica Silver-Greenberg, "Jeffrey Epstein Hoped to Seed Human Race with His DNA," *New York Times*, July 31, 2019, www.nytimes.com/2019/07/31/business/jeffrey-epstein-eugenics.html.

8. Nally, "Jeffrey Epstein, My Very, Very Sick Pal."

9. Steve Eder and Matthew Goldstein, "Jeffrey Epstein's Charity: An Image Boost Built on Deception," *New York Times*, Nov. 26, 2019, www.nytimes.com/2019/11/26/business/jeffrey-epstein-charity.html.

10. Eder and Goldstein, "Jeffrey Epstein's Charity."

11. Nick Bryant, "Here Is Pedophile Billionaire Jeffrey Epstein's Little Black Book," *Gawker*, Jan. 23, 2015, gawker.com/here-is-pedophile-billionaire-jeffrey-epsteins-little-b-1681383992.

12. "Who Was Jeffrey Epstein Calling? A Close Study of His Circle—Social, Professional, Transactional—Reveals a Damning Portrait of Elite New York," *New York*, July 22, 2019, nymag.com/intelligencer/2019/07/jeffrey-epstein-high-society-contacts.html.

13. Martin Gould, "Houseman Who Cleaned Jeffrey Epstein's Sex Toys Takes Secrets to Grave," *Daily Mail*, Jan. 6, 2015, www.dailymail.co.uk/news/article-2897939/Houseman-cleaned-pedophile-Jeffrey-Epstein-s-sex-toys-feared-billionaire-make-disappear-takes-secrets-grave.html.

14. Joe Pompeo, "Decoding Jeffrey Epstein's Mysterious, Star-Studded Black Book," *Vanity Fair*, July 18, 2019, www.vanityfair.com/news/2019/07/jeffrey -epstein-black-book-nick-bryant.

CHAPTER 15: THE MEDIA

1. Trilby Beresford, "'Sex and the City' Author on Middle-Aged Romance and Getting Kicked Out of Jeffrey Epstein's Home," *Hollywood Reporter*, July 29, 2019, www.hollywoodreporter.com/news/sex-city-author-middle-aged -romance-jeffrey-epstein-1226532.
2. Jesse Kornbluth, "I Was a Friend of Jeffrey Epstein; Here's What I Know," *Salon*, July 9, 2019, www.salon.com/2019/07/09/i-was-a-friend-of-jeffrey-epstein-heres -what-i-know/.
3. Maureen O. Connor, "Peggy Siegal Sends Her Regrets," *Vanity Fair*, Jan. 21, 2020, www.vanityfair.com/hollywood/2020/01/peggy-siegal-sends-her-regrets.
4. Cathy Burke, "Prince Andrew Tours Manhattan with Billionaire Sex Offender Jeffrey Epstein," *New York Post*, Feb. 21, 2011, nypost.com/2011/02/21/prince -andrew-tours-manhattan-with-billionaire-sex-offender-jeffrey-epstein/.
5. Connor, "Peggy Siegal Sends Her Regrets."
6. Tiffany Hsu, "Jeffrey Epstein Pitched a New Narrative. These Sites Published It," *New York Times*, July 21, 2019, www.nytimes.com/2019/07/21/business /media/jeffrey-epstein-media.html.
7. Vicky Ward, "I Tried to Warn You About Sleazy Billionaire Jeffrey Epstein in 2003," *Daily Beast*, Jan. 6, 2015, www.thedailybeast.com/i-tried-to-warn-you -about-sleazy-billionaire-jeffrey-epstein-in-2003.
8. David Carr, "Post-mortems for a Media Deal Undone," *New York Times*, Dec. 22, 2003, www.nytimes.com/2003/12/22/business/media-post-mortems-for-a -media-deal-undone.html.
9. David Carr, "Radar Magazine Lines Up Financing," *New York Times*, Oct. 19, 2004, www.nytimes.com/2004/10/19/arts/radar-magazine-lines-up-financing .html.
10. Katharine Q. Seelye, "Three Issues into New Life, Radar Magazine Is Being Shut Again," *New York Times*, Dec. 15, 2005, www.nytimes.com/2005/12/15/business /media/three-issues-into-new-life-radar-magazine-is-being-shut.html.
11. Joe Pompeo, "What the Media Knew About Epstein, the Monster Hiding in Plain Sight," *Vanity Fair*, July 10, 2019, www.vanityfair.com/news/2019/07 /manhattan-media-remembers-jeffrey-epstein.
12. "Jack Abramoff: The Lobbyist's Playbook," *60 Minutes*, CBS, May 30, 2012, www.cbsnews.com/news/jack-abramoff-the-lobbyists-playbook-30-05-2012/.

CHAPTER 16: THE ARREST

1. Benjamin Weiser, "Before Arrest, Jeffrey Epstein Was Seen with Girls Exiting His Jet," *New York Times*, Sept. 16, 2019, www.nytimes.com/2019/09/16/nyregion/jeffrey-epstein-investigation.html.
2. Philip Weiss, "The Fantasist: A Sex-Crime Investigation Reveals Jeffrey Epstein's Dangerous Dream World," *New York*, Dec. 7, 2007, nymag.com/news/features/41826/.
3. Landon Thomas Jr., "Jeffrey Epstein: International Moneyman of Mystery," *New York*, Oct. 29, 2002, nymag.com/nymetro/news/people/n_7912/.
4. vicourts.hosted.civiclive.com/common/pages/DisplayFile.aspx?itemId=16364025.
5. David Enrich and Jo Becker, "Jeffrey Epstein Moved Money Overseas in Transactions His Bank Flagged to U.S.," *New York Times*, July 23, 2019, www.nytimes.com/2019/07/23/business/jeffrey-epstein-deutsche-bank.html.
6. Tom Winter and David K. Li, "Jeffrey Epstein Had Cash, Diamonds, and a Foreign Passport Stashed in Safe, Prosecutors Say," NBC News, July 15, 2019, www.nbcnews.com/news/us-news/jeffrey-epstein-had-cash-diamonds-foreign-passport-stashed-safe-prosecutors-n1029851.
7. casetext.com/case/united-states-v-epstein-23.

CONCLUSION

1. Mary Hanbury, "L Brands CEO Steps Down as Company Sells Majority Share in Victoria's Secret," *Business Insider*, Feb. 20, 2020, www.businessinsider.com/l-brands-ceo-steps-down-company-sells-majority-share-in-victorias-secret-2020-2/.
2. Thornton McEnery, "Billionaire Glenn Dubin Retiring from Hedge Fund amid Fury over Jeffrey Epstein Ties," *New York Post*, Jan. 24, 2020, nypost.com/2020/01/24/billionaire-glenn-dubin-retiring-from-hedge-fund-amid-fury-over-jeffrey-epstein-ties/.
3. Spencer Neale, "Cindy McCain Admits 'We All Knew' About Epstein," *Washington Examiner*, Jan. 24, 2020, www.washingtonexaminer.com/news/cindy-mccain-admits-we-all-knew-about-epstein.

Printed in the United States
by Baker & Taylor Publisher Services